INVITATION TO EXIST

INVITATION TO EXISTENTIAL PSYCHOLOGY

A Psychology for the Unique Human Being and Its Applications in Therapy

Bo Jacobsen

Department of Sociology, The University of Copenhagen

BICENTENNIAL
1807
WILEY
2007
BICENTENNIAL

John Wiley & Sons, Ltd

Other Wiley Editorial Offices

John Wiley & Sons Inc., 111 River Street, Hoboken, NJ 07030, USA

Jossey-Bass, 989 Market Street, San Francisco, CA 94103-1741, USA

Wiley-VCH Verlag GmbH, Boschstr. 12, D-69469 Weinheim, Germany

John Wiley & Sons Australia Ltd, 42 McDougall Street, Milton, Queensland 4064, Australia

John Wiley & Sons (Asia) Pte Ltd, 2 Clementi Loop #02-01, Jin Xing Distripark, Singapore 129809

John Wiley & Sons Canada Ltd, 6045 Freemont Blvd, Mississauga, ONT, L5R 4J3, Canada

Wiley also publishes its books in a variety of electronic formats. Some content that appears in print
may not be available in electronic books.

Anniversary Logo Design: Richard J. Pacifico

Library of Congress Cataloging in Publication Data

Jacobsen, Bo.
  Invitation to existential psychology : a psychology for the unique human being and its
  applications in therapy / Bo Jacobsen.
    p.   cm.
  Includes bibliographical references and index.
  ISBN 978-0-470-02897-1 (ppc : alk. paper)—ISBN 978-0-470-02898-8 (pbk. : alk. paper)
  1. Existential psychology.   I. Title.
  BF204.5.J33 2007
  150.19′2—dc22
                                                                                        2007039288

British Library Cataloguing in Publication Data

A catalogue record for this book is available from the British Library

ISBN 978-0-470-02897-1 (ppc)
ISBN 978-0-470-02898-8 (pbk)

Typeset in 10/12pt Palatino by Integra Software Services Pvt. Ltd, Pondicherry, India

CONTENTS

ABOUT THE AUTHOR

Bo Jacobsen is professor at the Centre for Research in Existence and Society at the University of Copenhagen, Department of Sociology. His research specialisation is in Existential Psychology. He holds two doctorate degrees and has been in charge of several research projects on psychological and existential problems, for instance an intensive qualitative study on the psychological problems and existential reflections of cancer patients. He is also a practicing psychologist and an existential psychotherapist and supervisor. He has authored numerous articles and books on psychological and existential issues, all written in an incisive and engaging style. He has lectured on existential psychology and psychotherapy in London and throughout Continental Europe. His mission is to develop the human and existential dimensions of psychology and psychotherapy. In this way he aims to stimulate human beings to develop their openness and reach out for each other.

PREFACE

This book is an invitation to explore the richness and depth of the human being as seen by existential psychology. Psychology is not just for diagnosing psychological illnesses. Psychology also has to show people how it is possible to develop a fuller being, to achieve a more vibrant sense of being alive, to meet adversity, to get closer to states of happiness and love, and to acknowledge what is good and bad in their lives.

Existential psychology emphasises the specifically human dimensions of our life; that is, the ways in which we human beings are different from animals. We certainly have a body and contain a multitude of biological processes. What makes us human, however, is not our biology. We are made human by our gift of being able to *reflect* on our biology, as well as on every other aspect of our lives; to *talk about* these issues with each other; and to *decide* what kind of life we wish to live in consort with our fellow human beings.

One significant trend in recent psychology, psychiatry and therapy is the focus on brain waves, neurotransmitters and the repair of clear-cut diagnostic states. All this has its place. Yet the essence of being human remains that our anxieties, our pain and our disturbances as well as our joy and our potentialities are all woven into one unified structure: our own lives. Our so-called pathologies are intimately entwined with our resources, our plans and goals, the way we find meaning in our lives and the way we respond to life's big questions.

Existential psychology focuses on the existential life questions or life dilemmas that present themselves with greater and greater urgency in our time: How do we live meaningful lives? Is it possible to experience love and happiness in this world? How do we cope with loneliness? Can we trust our fellow human beings? How do we deal with crisis, adversity and losses when they happen? How will we know that we are doing the right thing when we make our basic choices and commitments? And where can we find the confidence, the courage and the determination to persevere throughout life in the way that is right for us?

The book is about the dilemmas and challenges of human life. Each chapter (except Chapter 1) will focus on one of life's crucial dilemmas, present concepts for describing it, theories for understanding it and examples illustrating what the dilemma is about and how we can meet this specific challenge in our own life and – if we are professionals helping other people – in the lives of our clients or patients. The book also aims to show how these basic dilemmas have different expressions in different societies and cultures, and that different ways of dealing with these dilemmas each have their own value.

The book is an invitation to reflect on your own life, but at the same time it is an attempt at developing a firmer framework for the discipline of existential psychology. In fact, we have three existential disciplines building upon each other in a logical way: existential philosophy, existential psychology and existential therapy.

The philosophical and the therapeutic disciplines are both represented by a number of recognised works that define the discipline in question. The discipline of existential psychology, however, has its concepts, theories and empirical basis scattered in a much more piecemeal manner throughout the extant literature, often delivered with a mix of philosophical and therapeutic principles. Sometimes expositions of existential therapy even jump directly from philosophy to therapy without specifying the psychological concepts and theories that actually underpin the therapeutic thinking and bridge the transition from philosophy to therapy. My ambition with this book is to single out these psychological elements and to present them as a whole, coherently and clearly.

My way of analysing psychological theory was influenced by my former teachers, professors Franz From and Johan Asplund. My initiation into philosophy took place as a Research Fellow at Cambridge University under Professor Paul Hirst, while my training in existential therapy was supervised by John Smidt Thomsen, Emmy van Deurzen and Ernesto Spinelli. I have learned so many important things from each of these eminent scholars and therapists. Thank you so much.

The book would not have come to life without the vigorous and continuous support of my research staff, Hanne Bess Boelsbjerg, Søren la Cour and Lisbeth W. Sørensen, and without the help of my language consultant, Mark Hebsgaard. I am most grateful for your contributions. Above all, I want to thank my wife, Else Østlund Jacobsen for her inspiration and for being the person she is.

Bo Jacobsen
Centre for Research in Existence and Society
University of Copenhagen
May 2007

CHAPTER 1

WHAT IS EXISTENTIAL PSYCHOLOGY?

EXISTENTIAL PSYCHOLOGY

Existential psychology is the branch of psychology that deals with each human being's relationship to the most essential life dilemmas, the so-called big questions of life. Existential psychology also aims to capture the spirit and feeling of life itself rather than subsuming life under a system of logical and systematic categories. Furthermore, existential psychology aims to include basic philosophical reflections in our psychological understanding, at the same time constituting the foundation for existential therapy, counselling and coaching.

Existential psychology is truly a branch of psychology proper; that is, a field of research with concepts and theories about the world that may be validated or refuted empirically. It certainly builds on existential philosophy, which may be defined as our basic thinking about life and the conditions governing life. Using this philosophy as a foundation, existential psychology is the sum total of concepts, theories and empirical knowledge that tells us how human beings interact with the big issues of life and how the basic conditions governing life emerge and are dealt with in everyday life situations. The main application of existential psychology at present lies within therapy. Existential therapy explicitly invites the client or patient to find their feet when confronted with the most important life issues.

So, there are three existential disciplines building upon each other: philosophy, psychology and therapy. Psychology is the body of knowledge that leads you from philosophy to therapy. You do not need to be an 'existentialist', a term used in a wide variety of ways, in order to profit from the fertile insights of existential psychology. You just need an open mind.

THE REAL PERSON AND THE ROLE OF PHENOMENOLOGY

Mainstream psychology imposes a large number of categories on life. These categories constitute the spectacles through which we observe human life.

Thus within the realms of clinical psychology and psychotherapy, we are not primarily trained in observing specific human beings in all their individuality and complexity. Rather, we are taught to observe cases of 'Panic Anxiety', 'Obsessive-Compulsive Disorder', 'Dysthymic Disorder' and 'Somatisation' as outlined in the ICD or DSM diagnostic systems.

Within the psychology of personality, we are urged to look for the so-called 'big five'; that is, five broad dimensions of traits according to which the human personality is said to be organised: Extraversion, Agreeableness, Conscientiousness, Neuroticism and Openness to experience (John & Srivastura, 1999, pp. 102ff).

It is often useful to classify, but how can psychologists, psychiatrists and other therapists learn to see unique individuals rather than types? This is where phenomenology comes in. Phenomenology observes or experiences the phenomena as they appear in themselves; that is, it ventures beyond the many ideas, stereotypes and images that we carry with us and impose on the phenomena we meet. Phenomenology is to meet the phenomenon in itself. You try to perceive the other person as they really are, the real person, without taking anything for granted. Look at this example:

> A nurse was looking in on an old man in a nursing home shortly before Christmas. 'So, Mr Smith, where are you going to celebrate Christmas this year?' she asked encouragingly while she washed him. 'Here'. Mr Smith's answer was cross and morose as usual. 'Well', she continued supportively, 'then perhaps someone will come and visit you here?'. 'No!' was the answer.
>
> The nurse felt both enraged and astounded. She knew for a fact that the old man had seven brothers and sisters living in neighbouring towns. Many of them could easily have put him up on Christmas Eve. She contacted his GP, who got angry and started phoning the man's family. He finally got hold of a sister: 'Oh, we would so much like to have him and we invited him a long time ago, but he would rather celebrate Christmas on his own in the nursing home. What are we going to do?'

What we observe here is a committed and competent nurse who is convinced that she *knows* what her patient wants: she does not need to ask him. According to phenomenology, however, we never know what another person wants, not even our own spouse or child. We have to ask and listen carefully.

When two people talk to each other, each of them usually makes assumptions about the world-view of the other person: I tend to assume that I look at the world in the same way as the other person. This tendency is particularly strong when the conversation has to do with life's meaning and values. Many misunderstandings arise when people in different life situations or from different cultural backgrounds meet. We also see this pattern in professional conversations.

Phenomenology breaks up this pattern. A phenomenological conversation will – as I show later – usually make a person feel deeply understood and well received. The person will come to life because the authentic, detailed rendering of his or her life experience will lead that person to unfold and become present in the room as he or she really is.

Phenomenology was originally an important philosophical school, founded by Edmund Husserl and further developed by Maurice Merleau-Ponty, Martin Heidegger and a number of other prominent philosophers during the first half of the twentieth century. We can understand the world correctly only when we include the observing subject in our thinking. That is one tenet of this philosophical approach. The world is not just there – not without us. We can understand ourselves or another human being only if we acknowledge that we human beings exist solely in our relatedness to the world. We do not exist in isolation (Heidegger, 1926, pp. 58–63; Merleau-Ponty, 1945, pp. 491–492).

The philosophy of phenomenology later gave rise to methods and approaches for the empirical disciplines of sociology, psychology and anthropology; as well as for the applied fields of psychotherapy and counselling.

In psychology, the phenomenological research methods were specifically developed by Amadeo Giorgi and his colleagues at the Duquesne University and Saybrook Graduate School in San Francisco. Giorgi founded the *Journal of Phenomenological Psychology*. In his book *Psychology as a human science* (Giorgi, 1970), Giorgi argues that psychology should belong to the human sciences, not to the natural sciences. He criticises the psychology of his time for its tendency to determine its contents by what can be measured rather than by the significance of the topic, meaning that topics like crying, laughing, friendship and love remain essentially unexamined. He speaks, characteristically, about the human sciences rather than the humanities: His goal is to unite the humanities with rigorous science. The road to this unity lies in phenomenology.

In psychotherapy and counselling, the application of phenomenology has been demonstrated by Ernesto Spinelli in a series of case stories (Spinelli, 1997). Spinelli points out three special rules of the phenomenological method when used in psychology and therapy:

1. Put your expectations and preconceptions as a psychologist or therapist in parenthesis and openly embrace the specific world presented by the client. This rule is called *the rule of parenthesis* or the *epoché* rule.

2. Describe, do not explain; do away with all explanations and all causal thinking and describe, describe, describe as concretely, down-to-earth and in as much detail as at all possible. This is *the rule of description*. For instance, ask the client to describe in detail the situation in which they live or how

they feel today or right now, but do not ask them to conjure up causal factors for their present misery.

3. When your description includes several elements, you should avoid emphasising any one element for as long as possible. Do not highlight any of the elements as particularly important. Let all elements be equally significant for as long as possible, lest you prematurely impose a pattern on the material. What is important will emerge when the time is ripe. This rule is called *the rule of horizontalisation* or the rule of equivalisation (Spinelli, 2005, pp. 19ff).

Throughout this book, I will present a number of illustrations that demonstrate how the phenomenological approach can be fruitful in understanding essential psychological phenomena such as happiness, love and loneliness. Phenomenology is also an important way of accepting and respecting cultural differences. Our basic life questions and life dilemmas, as described by existential psychology, have different cultural expressions that all deserve a precise description.

CAN PSYCHOLOGY BE ABOUT LIFE ITSELF?

Many psychologists, psychiatrists, therapists and counsellors enter their chosen field because they are attracted by the pulsating and varied nature of human life. They are fascinated by sensing the many unique ways in which human beings can unfold their lives. They love to relate to others and to help them unravel from their misery and redirect their lives in a more constructive direction.

These professionals need a body of psychological knowledge and understanding that respects their interest in specific human lives without reducing these lives to abstract categories, cause-and-effect relationships and statistical averages.

Amadeo Giorgi proposes the term *life world* as the crux of such a psychology. The relationships between living persons and the worlds in which they live should be the central focus; hence, all phenomena that we study must be understood as involving both the individual and the surrounding world (Giorgi, 1970, pp. 17ff). Earlier in the history of psychology, a similar intellectual project was carried out by the outstanding psychologist Kurt Lewin. In his so-called field theory, Lewin wanted to conceptualise 'the life space, containing the person and his psychological environment' (Lewin, 1938, p. 2).

Whether we talk about life worlds or life space, our language makes it quite difficult to convey the person–world connection of human beings, because our language disunites the totality into a subject and an object. It is almost impossible to write about 'unfolding your life' or 'realising your potentialities' without presenting the image of an isolated and delimited individual. The description conjures up an image of an individual that occasionally connects with other things and persons, but who is fundamentally alone. The very idea of a person who makes choices, lives through crises, relates to death and finds meaning in life is difficult to describe without at the same time evoking the notion of a person with a delimited body and a delimited psyche.

This is not how the life-world totality of a human being is in fact made up. Human beings are always in relationships – we live in them and through them. We are nurtured by them and produce through them; everything that a human being gives and receives, from birth until death, evolves through relationships. Probably we are nothing other than the combined sum of our relationships, and, once we have entered into them, our relationships cannot be done away with. Even if we decide never again to see someone who was once close to us, we will carry the relationship with us in our future life.

Medard Boss suggests abolishing the term 'psyche' to signify the seat of our mental faculties (Boss, 1994, Ch 8). Instead, he speaks of the person's *being-in-the-world*. The notion of the other person as a being-in-the-world sums up the crucial person–world connection, but it quickly becomes linguistically clumsy. When you read the following pages, please keep in mind that our language forces the author to focus on the person and the life process as such, making it difficult to account for the contexts in which our lives are continuously unfolding. The text presents the basic life concepts as if they resided within the individual. Please remember, however, that life feeling, life courage and life energy always develop in continuous interaction with the world.

THREE BASIC LIFE CONCEPTS: LIFE FEELING, LIFE COURAGE AND LIFE ENERGY

Life Feeling

Sometimes you are flooded with a poignant sensation of really being alive. At other times you feel tired, heavy, bored or dead. Most people have a strong preference for the sense of being alive, so it should be interesting to explore what characterises such life-world situations. In an interview study conducted by the author, a number of people were asked this question:

> Sometimes one feels full of energy or particularly alive. Can you describe a situation in which you have felt particularly alive?

The results were summarised like this:

Some people feel particularly alive in connection with *practical and other physical tasks*. A man who has recently moved into a new house together with his wife says: 'Now I really feel like keeping things neat and tidy (...) once in a while, I do the window sills and clean the windows. And just the other day, I cleaned the bathroom (...) With our new house, I really feel like doing something.'

Sports activities make some people feel particularly alive. A former carpenter used to bike race as a young man. His motto was: 'I can, I must and I will...and then I won,' he says. 'The longer the race was, the harder it was, the better it was for me (...) I wasn't afraid to use my strength. And my body! It just felt so good doing it.'

Others feel particularly alive when they are in *social relationships*, among family and friends. A grandmother of three says: 'I always feel particularly alive when my grandchildren come to visit, especially when the little one comes (...) when Laura is here, you just have to be particularly alive because she's doing so many crazy things.' Another woman emphasises the feeling that other people need her; that she has something to give. Then she feels alive: 'It gives me an enormous kick, you can feel that you are bloody well alive (...) there is someone who actually needs you.'

Still others feel alive when focused on their *own inner being*. They may experience their own inner processes both bodily and mentally. A man has begun to practice Tai Chi. When he is doing this, he feels particularly alive: 'The first time I was in the Tai Chi-room, I felt that I was bubbling with life (...) I felt a lot of energy (...) I actually felt a tingling from the soles of my feet and all the way up...and I thought, "My God, how wonderful it is to be alive." I really felt that.' A woman describes how, after she fell ill, she has developed a special inner feeling of being alive. 'Even if I won a million dollars I wouldn't feel as alive as I did on Easter morning when I went for a walk alone (...) I feel all bubbly inside. And really feel at one with life.'

Finally, some people feel alive *outdoors*. A woman says: 'When I'm in contact with nature or when I'm out at sea, then I feel particularly alive. Especially now, during the summer holidays. We stayed in a summer cottage by the sea, and that made me feel very much alive (...) My thoughts seem extremely clear. I feel good. I think it's the water and the vast expanse.'

Someone else says: 'I simply got new energy from being at the seaside. To lie down on the beach and to have the wild wind blow warm sand on my body, and then to throw myself into the waves. To sit and watch the sunset every evening. That was new energy for me. Life energy means that I can get up in the morning and feel joy over my existence. Just knowing that I'm here.'

Other respondents talk about living intensely when they are involved in their work projects, or when they are reading, travelling, doing voluntary social work, being with their beloved, fishing, gardening and a multitude of other activities. Perhaps each human being has their special world of activity and unfolding, their special space for intense living. We all have situations in which we feel alive with particular intensity. At the other end of the scale, people may even feel that they do not live at all. They feel dead inside. They may even feel that life has come to a complete standstill and will not commence until they do something else or go live with someone else.

However, whether we feel more or less alive at any given moment, as human beings we all have an idea about what *it means* for us – in our own lives – to be more or less alive.

So what is at the core of feeling alive? Rollo May describes what he calls the *'I-am'-experience* (May, 1983, pp. 99ff). It is the spontaneous experience of just being here. Simply because I am here, I also have the right to be here, the right to exist. I experience my own being and develop life feeling. If a person can spontaneously experience that they live, they will thereby get to know their own basic values. Opinions about good and bad, right and wrong are not just taken over from parents and society: They grow organically out of our selves.

Ronald D Laing has also described an aspect of our life feeling. He has coined the term 'ontological security' and the antonym 'ontological insecurity' (Laing, 1965, pp. 39ff). A person can have a sense of their being in the world as a real, alive and whole person who lives in temporal continuity. This person can step forward and meet others with clarity. Laing calls such a person ontologically secure. They, says Laing, will meet the trials of life on the basis of a firm feeling of their own and other people's identity and reality.

In psychotic states we see the opposite: a lack of existential foundation. In these states we find individuals who feel fundamentally unreal, not alive, not whole and with unclear boundaries.

Also Jon Kabat-Zinn in his work on stress and meditation captures the phenomenon of life feeling. He teaches his patients 'to taste their own wholeness as they are, right now (…) to accept ourselves right now, as we are, symptoms or no symptoms, pain or no pain, fear or no fear' (Kabat-Zinn, 1990, pp. 279–280).

The above examples of feeling alive are expressions of life feeling in its purest form. In some of them, other elements such as the need to perform or the need to be loved are admixed with the quintessential life feeling. But in all of them, the life feeling is lucid; reading the examples, you sense the nurturing and healing nature of these experiences.

Life Courage

Life feeling is an important component in life courage. But the courage to live encompasses more than life feeling, pure and simple. According to Paul Tillich, existential theologian and philosopher, life courage, that is the courage to be, is a phenomenon comprising both a natural component (something that is part of living in itself) and a moral component (something that one strives for). The courage to live is a conscious attitude in which one affirms one's being alive in spite of what works against this basic affirmation of life. The opposites are fear and anxiety. Courage is 'the power of the mind to overcome fear' (Tillich, 1980, p. 34). In other words, the courage to live is equivalent to choosing to live: *to add one's power of decision to the natural life process.*

Courage fights against fear and anxiety. Courage can easily pinpoint fear, which is manifestly directed towards an object. Anxiety, which lacks a definite object, is more difficult to isolate. The basic struggle of the human being thus stands between anxiety and courage. And the anxiety in question is existential anxiety.

According to Tillich, *existential anxiety* assumes three forms, each of them interconnected and each leading to the other. The most basic form is anxiety of fate and death. This anxiety threatens the individual's sense of having the right to exist. The second form is anxiety of emptiness and meaninglessness. This type of anxiety threatens the spiritual dimensions of the individual, as well as the individual's longing for meaning. The third form is anxiety of guilt and condemnation. This type of anxiety threatens the moral identity of the individual (Tillich, 1980, pp. 40ff).

These three forms of existential anxiety belong within the normal spectrum. Pathological anxiety is a distortion of these forms. If a human being lacks the courage to confront their existential anxiety, they may flee into neurosis. Such a person will tend to abandon living freely and openly by building up rigid patterns of defence, security and perfection.

Many of the anxiety states that ordinary people struggle with in their everyday lives and present in the consultation rooms of doctors and psychologists may be fruitfully understood on the basis of Tillich's three types of existential anxiety: (1) the anxiety of a patient with chronic pain; (2) the sense of emptiness of somebody who has recently been divorced; or (3) the feeling of being condemned experienced by the assault victim – all of these examples may be understood meaningfully as existential anxiety according to Tillich's categories. Pathological anxiety, says Tillich, is a result of the person's inability to confront their existential anxiety (Tillich, 1980, p. 77). If the doctor or the psychologist tries to reduce a state of anxiety to a limited condition that should be removed from the person, they will also tend to impair the life quality of that person, because they risk removing the existential rootedness of the individual along with the anxiety. This is why it is so important to combine the frequently used cognitive-behavioural therapy with an existential perspective (see Hayes *et al.*, 1999). It is, of course, even more important that any medical treatment of anxiety should be combined with a therapeutic session delving into existential discussion.

Existential anxiety cannot be removed; it belongs to and is part of life itself. But existential anxiety adds an essential contribution of its own to life, namely the quality of *self-affirmation* that it invokes. Anxiety has the unexpected quality of bringing about individual fortitude. Let us compare this with the way in which bacteria elicit the production of valuable antibodies that would otherwise not have been developed. The bacteria call forth antibodies; they in turn provide resilience. Anxiety sparks self-affirmation, which is then transformed into courage, turning people into courageous beings in the process (Tillich, 1980, pp. 32ff).

Hence life courage may be defined as a fundamental, spontaneous *life feeling* combined with a consciously chosen *courage to live*, developed through the confrontation with existential anxiety. *Life courage is a basic mood or attunement in a person that tells us about this person's wish to live, their basic character, and their will to face life's challenges and difficulties.*

Life Energy (Vitality)

Among the seriously ill, we encounter a phenomenon that nobody can explain. A doctor may have two patients with the same ailment, a fatal disease. They have the disease in approximately the same degree and the doctor's prognosis is that they both have about six months left to live. Subsequently, one patient fades and dies quickly, while the other perks up inexplicably, developing their own healing resources and surviving perhaps another 10 years.

In medical literature, patients who defy all negative prognoses are called 'exceptional patients'. But why do some wane before their time while others seem to resuscitate themselves? What is it that makes some people cave in when faced with moderate adversity while others persevere despite the most unbelievable difficulties?

By the term *life energy* or *vitality* we understand the ability of the organism *to survive*. Life energy is an organismic variable. While life courage is a basic attunement that can be experienced from within, life energy is a trait that can be observed from the outside. Based on certain signs in a human being or other organism, an observer will get an impression of high or low life energy.

> A neonatal ward occasionally receives infants with a foetal age of 5–6 months. For some days, these premature children hover between life and death. Doctors and nurses observe them and speculate on who among them will survive. They often use words like life force, life energy and the will to live: This infant will probably live, even though he is among the youngest. That one would die, they thought, but life still remained strong in the organism. That infant had an unexpected amount of life energy.

From the moment they are born, human infants are endowed with varying amounts of life energy or vitality. This life energy seems to stay with the children as they grow up. This does not mean to say that it is purely biologically or genetically determined. There is every reason to believe that psychological and sociocultural factors codetermine the magnitude of the life force, and increasingly so during the course of life.

This life force determines the expectations of survival of an adult suffering from a fatal disease and the length of the lifespan of an older person.

How may we understand the nature of life energy? There are two opposing views:

On the one hand, life energy may be seen as a *purely biological phenomenon*. Different dandelions have different height, strength and powers of survival. Dogs and horses have different sizes, strength and powers of survival. Human beings, too, are born with different sizes, strength and powers of survival and, consequently, with different vitality. The biological view is supported by the genetic fact that longevity seems to run in families.

On the other hand, life energy is also viewed as an *existential* or *bio-spiritual phenomenon*. The biological level and the spiritual level are united in the realm of existence. By the spiritual level we understand the human being's search for a higher meaning. One advocate of this view is Paul Tillich. Tillich sees the life courage mentioned above as an expression of the person's vitality. Decreasing vitality leads to decreasing courage, and strengthened vitality provides strengthened courage. Neurotic individuals, he says, lack vitality; in other words, they lack biological substance.

Vitality derives not only from the biological level, says Tillich. The vitality emanating from a human being's life cannot be separated from the goals and purposes of that being. Vitality and intentionality are mutually interdependent.

Human beings can transcend any given situation and thereby create something beyond themselves. The more they possess of this creative force, the more vitality they have. In other words, the biological dimensions of humankind are interwoven in a structure of meaning. 'Vitality', says Tillich, 'is not something which can be separated from the totality of man's being, his language, his creativity, his spiritual life, his ultimate concern' (Tillich, 1980, p. 82).

Tillich thus understands vitality as a bio-spiritual phenomenon. Its force comes from the biological and the spiritual levels alike and these levels mingle in the world of existence.

Bio-energetic therapists and other therapists that work with bodily touch often state that they are in direct contact with the life energy or vitality of the client. In spite of the prefix 'bio', many therapists belonging to these schools find that the life energy they stimulate and work with is not entirely biological in nature. They describe the currents of energy as having a more spiritual, cosmic or in other ways strangely lucid character (Boadella, 1987).

Hence the view that life energy is a purely biological phenomenon will not stand against an existential analysis. Even though biological forces are very active indeed in human life, the actions that spring from them always form part of a meaningful social context. Human beings cannot function without goal, meaning and intention. Furthermore, the biological forces are always integrated in a mental frame of reference.

Existentially, life energy must be viewed as bio-spiritual, as a force that integrates biology with what is spiritual and meaningful. Life energy does not remain the same throughout the course of a human lifetime. Much seems to indicate that around the time of birth, life energy is predominantly biological, but also influenced by love and interpersonal contact. Later on, vitality is increasingly transformed into something more specifically marked by the life meaning and life tasks that are unique to each human being, even though it is sustained by a strong biological component throughout life.

In Box 1.1, we summarise our discussion by juxtaposing the three basic concepts of human life processes.

Box 1.1   Three Basic Life Concepts

Life feeling is the person's spontaneous sense of being alive, being coherent and sensing a right to be here.

Life courage is the person's life feeling combined with their determination to conquer fear and anxiety in order to carry out their life project.

Life energy or *vitality* is the ability of the organism to survive even under difficult circumstances and to achieve longevity. Here, the biological component is strong, but our biology is woven into patterns of meaning and intention that codetermine our life energy.

THE BIG QUESTIONS OF LIFE

Some animals seem to live an easy life. A dog or a cat, for example, may spend its whole life eating, sleeping, wandering about, looking, listening, mating and resting. The life of an animal is a life without problems (although life for some animals is periodically unpleasant or momentarily painful). It is a life without reflections on life.

Human beings are compelled to live a life in which they reflect on their own life. All human beings experience moments when they have to choose between alternate courses of action. We all entertain thoughts about when we are going to die, or how we can achieve a desired goal. We also think about falling ill, getting older, being alone, having enemies and loved ones and about many other aspects of our lives.

As human beings, we are all doomed to reflect on our lives. But this requirement is also a great opportunity to develop ourselves towards higher states that definitely distinguish us from the animals.

According to existential theory, the life reflections we all undertake are not accidental and arbitrary. Although every individual entertains private thoughts about their own life, such thoughts are confined to certain themes that are important, yet limited in number.

Our thoughts on living all derive from the same source: the structure of existence into which we are born. This structure of existence revolves around a finite number of basic life conditions.

As human beings, our options are such that we can either close our eyes to these basic conditions and live falsely or blindly in some kind of make-believe life; or we can choose to look these existentials (for definition, see below) squarely in the eye and learn how to relate to them constructively, thus living more openly and freely, in a more grounded and real way. Existential psychologists use the word *authenticity* to designate this genuine life that is a possibility open to everyone.

The Structure of Existence

There are different catalogues and lists surveying these basic life conditions. The most well-known is Irvin Yalom's enumeration of four basic existential conditions: (1) that we are going to die; (2) that in decisive moments, we are alone; (3) that we have the freedom to choose our life; and (4) that we struggle to create meaning in a world in which our life meaning is not given beforehand (Yalom, 1980). According to Yalom, these four basic conditions constitute a structure that is our premise, something that all human beings are born into. The four conditions set the frame and the agenda for the life of each individual. Many people would rather avoid thinking about, talking about and relating to these basic conditions, including death, but this fact does not weaken their impact, rather the opposite.

Yalom assigns about the same status to these basic conditions as did Freud in his era to sexuality: a force that permeates almost everything and to which most people close their eyes, causing the force to make itself felt in a distorted form.

Another familiar theory about life's basic conditions, developed by Medard Boss, lists seven fundamental traits of human life: (1) human beings live in space; (2) human beings live in time; (3) human beings unfold through their body; (4) human beings live in a shared world; (5) human beings always live in a particular mood, a certain psychological atmosphere; (6) human beings live in a historic context; and (7) human beings live with the awareness of their own death (Boss, 1994, Ch 7).

These seven basic conditions may be called existentials, core factors in everybody's life. If we look at (2), it is true for all of us that as we live, time goes by. We all have a past, a present and a future; we all live at a specific intersection of the individual time axis that stipulates the beginning and end of each individual lifespan. We all have things that we choose to spend time doing and other things that we do not. It is true for all of us that we cannot use the same time twice. The moment you have read this sentence, it will never come back; a moment can be lived only once. All these temporal dimensions in our life are active and influence us whether we want to think about them or not. Evidence also suggests that we can live more freely and in a more enlightened way if we indeed choose to think about them.

Other existential authors have developed similar lists and overviews of humankind's basic life conditions (Bugental, 1987; Condrau, 1989). As early as half a century ago, however, one particularly interesting exposition was formulated by Erich Fromm, the German-American humanistic psychoanalyst and writer: 'All passions and strivings of man', he writes, 'are attempts to find an answer to his existence' (Fromm, 1956a, pp. 27ff). Fromm then goes on to mention as basic points the individual's fundamental need: (1) for love (relatedness); (2) for transcending oneself; (3) for developing rootedness and a feeling of being at home; (4) for finding one's identity; and (5) for finding one's orientation and meaning in life. According to Fromm, the most specific characteristics of any human being derive from the fact that *our bodily functions belong to the animal kingdom, whereas our mental and social lives belong to a human, conscious world that is aware of itself* (Fromm, 1956, pp. 22ff). Therefore, the satisfaction of our instinctual needs is not sufficient to make us happy. We constantly strive towards discovering new solutions to the rampant contradictions of our existence; towards finding ever higher forms of unity with nature, with our fellow human beings and with ourselves. The fact that even the most prosperous of the world's nations display such massive levels of alcoholism, crime, suicides, drug abuse and boredom testify to this.

The Basic Life Conditions Seen as Life Dilemmas

The basic categories of life conditions proposed by Irvin Yalom, Medard Boss, Erich Fromm and related scholars share many traits. The differences between them are not contradictory in nature, they are in fact supplementary (Jacobsen, 2003).

Irvin Yalom's four categories form the core of this book's structure, but I have expanded them to include dimensions from Medard Boss, Gion Condrau and

Erich Fromm. This theoretical synthesis has resulted in a system of six basic life conditions or life questions, presented below.

The basic life conditions are sometimes seen as relatively straightforward categories or realities, but each may also be viewed as a dilemma representing two opposite poles between which our life is torn and between which it must find a balance. I favour the latter view, seeing the basic conditions as dilemmas, because this view accentuates the choices we always face as human beings. Existential theorists subscribing to this view would suggest that there are a number of given *ontological facts* (e.g. that one day we will die), but that these facts present themselves to us in the form of *life dilemmas*.

In everyday language, we understand a dilemma as a situation in which we are faced with a difficult choice between two alternatives, A and B. You cannot have both at the same time.

By a *life dilemma* we understand a situation in which the choice stands between two poles that both fall within what we normally expect out of life. Both belong to what you perceive to be a reasonable or happy life. But you cannot see how you can reconcile them or integrate them. For some people, 'to be oneself' or 'to be with others' is such a dilemma. The life question you might stop and think about in such a situation is this: How can I find and define myself (something that I usually do on my own) and at the same time bond intimately with friends and loved ones? Existential psychology deals with that type of question. Existential therapy, as described by van Deurzen (2002) aims at helping the client face such dilemmas. Life questions are the questions that we human beings raise in relation to the life dilemmas.

For the purposes of this theoretical synthesis, the existential theories have been integrated into six basic life dilemmas and life questions. Each of them forms the content of one of the subsequent chapters of the book. Here they are, each formulated as life dilemmas and life questions:

1. *Happiness vs Suffering* (Chapter 2): How can I strive towards happiness when I know that my life will inevitably contain suffering?

2. *Love vs Aloneness* (Chapter 3): Is it possible to overcome my basic aloneness in a love relationship? Can I still be myself in a love relationship? And is it at all possible to find love in this world?

3. *Adversity vs Success* (Chapter 4): When I find myself in dire straits following an accident or a loss or some other serious life event, how can I deal with that situation in such a way that I will grow from it instead of shrinking and getting stuck?

4. *Death Anxiety vs Life Commitment* (Chapter 5): Knowing that death can arrive at any time, how can I transcend my anxiety and commit myself fully to life?

5. *Free Choice vs the Obligations of Your Life Reality* (Chapter 6): Given the physical, financial and social realities of my life and origin, which I did not ask for, how can I make these realities my own positive and constructive choice? And how can I create a worthwhile future life through my choices?

6. *Life Meaning vs Meaninglessness* (Chapter 7): Given the chaotic character of our present world, how may I define the meaning and values of my life and find a clear direction for it?

The dilemmas are interconnected. If, for instance, you are exposed to sudden adversity or deep suffering or somebody's sudden death you will very likely at the same time get into contact with your basic feeling of aloneness or with a sense of life's meaninglessness. And if you are lucky to experience deep love, you will very likely at the same time get a feeling of your life as being happy and meaningful. Such interconnections have been pointed out by Yalom (1980) and Condrau (1989) and many other existential authors. The interconnectedness stems from the fact that our basic ontology is universal and its implications for our existence therefore interrelated.

We are all torn between the opposites that constitute the six dilemmas mentioned above. You could even add the fundamental dilemma mentioned by Erich Fromm of uniting the biology-driven animal part and the conscious, cultural and spiritual part of our being. Am I primarily an animal? Or am I primarily a conscious, thinking, ethical being? And in what ways can I unite these poles? That could be seen as the seventh, foundational and overarching existential dilemma, governing all our lives as human beings.

How to navigate your way through the abovementioned dilemmas along a constructive path is what life is all about, and certainly what existential psychology is about.

To the extent that you succeed in finding your own two feet in relation to these life questions and dilemmas, to that extent, the existential psychologists would say, you live an authentic life.

WHAT IS IT TO LIVE AUTHENTICALLY?

As a human being you are confronted with a highly important choice concerning your own life. Either you can say, I'll do like everyone else, I'll do what others expect me to do, I'll try to *be* like the others. Or you can say, I believe there are some choices that are more important and more right or true for me than certain other choices. I must find out which are the important and right things for me to do and I will try to live accordingly.

In existential psychology, the latter choice is called *to live authentically*. Authentic means genuine or known to be true. To live authentically means to live truthfully; that is, in accordance with your own deep convictions, beliefs and values. Indeed, some writers would add: in accordance with yourself and your bodily nature and temperament. To live authentically also means to find your own two feet in relation to the basic life dilemmas mentioned above.

The existential philosopher and theologian John Macquarrie defines authenticity like this: Life is authentic to the extent that the individual has taken possession of their own self and moulded that self in their own image. Inauthentic existence is moulded by external factors, whether they are circumstances, moral codes, political and religious authorities, or other influences (Macquarrie, 1972, p. 206).

The existential definition of authentic living, says Macquarrie, has more to do with form than with content. It is *the shape* of the existence that counts, *the extent* to which it has achieved unity rather than being scattered, *the way* it exercises freedom and self-determination; rather than being determined by the prevailing tastes and standards (Macquarrie, 1972, p. 207). This does not imply that you cannot independently choose to live according to the prevailing tastes and standards. You can and some certainly do.

The moral philosopher Mary Warnock sees authenticity as each human being's ability to fulfil his or her own potential and possibilities. To live authentically is to recognise that each human being is unique and to accept the personal consequence that, this being so, one has to find one's very own determination and realise one's own potential (Warnock, 1970).

The existential therapist Hans Cohn encourages us not to see the concept of authenticity as a goal that can be achieved. All people are inauthentic at certain times; that is part of life (Cohn, 1993). Along similar lines, Martin Heidegger writes that the fact that existence is inauthentic does not mean that it entails less being or a lower level of being. At the same time, authenticity is of course something that is deeply desirable (Heidegger, 2000).

Many people seem to live in a somewhat superficial way for years. They buzz from one activity to the next, play the parts that are required of them, watch TV. They seem to forget the deeper meaning of life and do not appear to know clearly what they are here for. They mechanically perform in the roles and display the attitudes that they think that the others expect of them. When we direct our lives according to the expectations of the others, we live, says Heidegger, in order to follow the 'they' (in German: *das Man*).

Then at a certain point, some people may experience a sudden awakening, as if dramatically summoned to life. Heidegger talks about the call of conscience. When using this term, he does not mean the public conscience, the overall moral codes, but the conscience that comes from the depths of oneself. It is a call from the authentic part of oneself struggling to emerge, to come to life and summon the rest of oneself to life. According to Heidegger, this voice exhorts the person to take full responsibility for their own life (Heidegger, 2000, pp. 318ff).

How may you best take your own life seriously without at the same time being too burdened by this reflection? One answer is *resoluteness* (Deurzen-Smith, 1995, pp. 13–25). Resolute action is characterised by decisiveness, firmness and determination. Yes means yes, and no means no. Resoluteness means clarity and is often developed following difficult life experiences. The person knows what they want. Resoluteness is related to the person's ability to stay focused and concentrated.

> A woman in her late 50s has been through a crisis. Today she is alive, active and loving when she is with her family. 'Sometimes', she says, 'you simply love life.'
>
> Seventeen years ago her mother died suddenly and without warning. The woman cannot forgive herself that her mother died without their having had the opportunity to talk. 'It has influenced me in the sense that you shouldn't postpone anything. If you have something you want to finish, then you should finish it. Because there are no guarantees that you'll be here tomorrow (...) If there is something that I want to say to someone, I say it now (...) I never got to tell her that I love her more than anything in the world (...)'

To live with resoluteness or determination presupposes a certain clarity of mind as to what you are here for, what counts for you, what you stand for and what you are against. Such clarity is generally acquired by living through a certain number of difficult life situations. A few people seem to be born with this gift of clarity. But all the rest of us have to acquire this clarity of life the hard way. Afterwards, however, we find life incomparably more valuable. There seems to be no easy way to such clarity. For some reason, almost all of us live under the impression that other people have easier access to their accomplishments and results than we do ourselves. But this is usually a false impression.

Once you have acquired a minimum degree of clarity about what you are living for (a subject that is discussed throughout this book), the questions of authenticity and how to take your own life seriously do not appear to be 'heavy' questions. These questions need not weigh you down. It is possible to be authentic and spontaneous at the same time. Medard Boss, one of the fathers of existential therapy, conceives of the authentic life as a life marked by playfulness and humour. His concept of the ideal state of mind, *composed, joyous serenity*, entails ease and heaviness going hand in hand. Playfulness and seriousness embrace one another, as do our knowledge of death and our commitment to life.

Life Regrets and Authenticity

Most people seem to ask themselves quite often: How should my future be? Should I aim at this or that? In the same way, many people reflect upon their past. Some ruminate. Others discuss with their friends or their partners: Did I do the right things? Did I use my time and meet my challenges in the best possible way?

In an interview study, we put this question to a number of respondents:

> If you could live your life again, would you change anything or would you live it the same way?

Here are some answers:

'I would probably have liked to take more part in life (…) instead of sitting back like that (…) and not really dare to join in (…) I have sort of felt that it wasn't really my place to make demands on life (…)' (Woman, 38, secretary)

A woman worked 10 years in her husband's company and didn't like the administrative work in itself or working for her husband. 'It was probably the most stupid thing we ever did in our life together (…) I stayed out of a sense of convenience, right? And I can see that today, of course (…) that it was the most stupid thing (…)' (Woman, 47, former administrative officer)

'I would probably have lived (…) the life surrounded by nature that perhaps I wanted deep inside. Instead I flowed with the stream by haphazardly starting an education (…) And clearly, if I were to live a new life, I would much rather have stayed married to only one man (…) I think I regret that I married Frank. That is probably what I regret most of all (…) I have had to compromise too much (…)' This woman states that were she to live her life again, she would not marry Frank. Despite many good moments she feels that it was the wrong choice. But with two children, she was between a rock and a hard place, and then Frank was there, generous and with flowers. (Woman, 44, project manager)

As it turns out, all three respondents have had regrets, either occasioned by specific actions or a particular attitude or lifestyle.

Regrets of this type are rather common, but perhaps it takes a certain amount of courage to look them squarely in the eye. There are several ways of dealing with such regrets. Some see them as a fate they cannot change. Others see the dissatisfactions as something they can learn from; partly by correcting things for the remainder of their lives, partly by passing their lesson on to the next generation.

But not everyone is burdened by discontents:

'By and large, I would live my life in the same way. I do, however, feel bad about the people that I have somehow let down. I also regret that I didn't get enough out of my university studies, because I had too many other things going on in my life'. (Woman, 27, student)

'I would like to live my life again, on exactly the same terms. And that doesn't mean to say that my life has been the easiest of lives; it certainly hasn't. I haven't been spared anything (...) But if you take life as a whole, I would be prepared to take the good things with the bad one more time (...)' (Woman, 63, administrative executive)

'Well, no, I don't really think I would change anything. I think that I have lived a pretty good life; you know, nice and quiet (...) I have worked in the same place of employment for 43 years and so on and so forth; that seems very much to indicate that my whole life has been satisfactory (...)' (Man, 71, former mason, retired)

These people do not have any regrets gnawing away at their souls. Have they been on the right track all along and been able to stick to what was most important? Or have they been able to live with and accept the deficiencies and ailments that crop up in most lives, enabling them to truly take possession of their lives? We human beings seem to have two ways of coming to terms with former deficiencies: we can redirect our future life or we can condone our past.

Existential Guilt and Authenticity

In existential psychology, life regrets are seen as connected with a specific theory about guilt, the theory of existential guilt. In other schools of psychology and therapy, for example psychoanalysis or cognitive therapy, guilt is mainly seen as a pathological phenomenon and as a symptom that should be treated in some way. Irvin Yalom lists three types of guilt: real guilt, neurotic guilt and existential guilt (Yalom, 1980, p. 276). Real guilt arises if you have damaged another person in real life; if for instance in the process of backing your car into your garage, you crushed your neighbour's leg due to a moment's lack of attention. Neurotic guilt occurs if you have damaged someone only in your imagination. Say for instance that you have to decline your sister's birthday invitation. She perfectly understands, but you cannot let go of a deep, nagging feeling that you have let her down. Existential guilt is a positive element in people's life, as Rollo May also underlines (May, 1983, pp. 114–116). It points out the areas in which you have not as yet lived up to the possibilities that were offered to you, including the possibility to treat others and nature with care and respect. Therefore, although it may be painful, existential guilt is a chance to redirect the rest of your life and to reach some sort of reconciliation with that which cannot be changed.

Authenticity is difficult to define. The definition must be sufficiently open to embrace the fact that the term is infused with meaning by every living person in their own unique way. However, authenticity can be seen as one of the most fruitful and promising concepts in the realm of psychology, paving the way from the discipline of psychology to 'the good life'. This term allows practitioners applying psychological knowledge and psychological theories to demonstrate how psychology is not just for diagnosing maladaptations and psychological illnesses. Psychology also has to show people how it is possible to develop a more truthful life, to achieve a more vibrant sense of being alive, to develop more happiness, to experience love and to acknowledge what is good and bad in their lives.

WHAT MAKES EXISTENTIAL PSYCHOLOGY DIFFERENT?

Existential psychology distinguishes itself from other disciplines within psychology by requiring that the main focus of psychology must be human life and each individual's relation to life's basic conditions and most important questions.

What these big questions are and how they are related to life's everyday events, thoughts, feelings and pursuits will be the subject of the rest of this book. In a similar vein, existential therapy is a kind of therapy where the therapist – in a direct, attentive relationship – stimulates the client to find their own footing in relation to life's crucial questions. In Appendix B you will find a brief description of existential therapy.

Existential psychology and existential therapy have distinctive characteristics in relation to other schools of psychology and therapy. A number of these will be pointed out throughout the book.

Existential psychology differs significantly from mainstream psychology in its explicit focus on essential life questions as the most important subject matter of psychology and in its insistence on the phenomenological perspective. Therefore, psychology should primarily account for life as experienced from within rather than behaviour observed from without. This difference gives existential psychologists less 'safe' knowledge about people's reactions in, say, traffic situations or child development stages, but more understanding of the real aspirations and real-life problems of human beings. It should be noted that we are here talking about psychology as a subject and a research field comprising theoretical and empirical knowledge about human beings, not only in a natural science sense, but in a broader sense comprising social and human science perspectives (Giorgi, 1970, 2001; Schneider, 1998).

Compared with Freudian and Jungian psychology, there are a number of similarities concerning the psychologist's in-depth interest in the lives of individual human beings. An important difference, however, is that the psychoanalytic traditions attach considerable significance to the consequences of childhood events, whereas existential psychologists and therapists are more concerned with an individual's present and future state and with their continuous openness to change. Furthermore, existential psychologists and therapists do not propound interpretations 'behind the backs' of their clients, but advocate detailed descriptions of their life situations and life perspectives.

Compared with cultural and cross-cultural psychology, there are certain differences as to the emphasis placed on cultural variation. However, in the long run the two approaches should be able to complement each other and reach a state of integration.

Existential psychology is related to phenomenological psychology, humanistic psychology, positive psychology and to some of the narrative (social constructivist) trends in psychology. There are also certain differences here, as pointed out in Box 1.2 and in more detail throughout the book.

Box 1.2 Schools of Psychology (as seen from the point of view of Existential Psychology)

Existential Psychology

- Focuses on essential life dilemmas and the big questions of life
- Emphasises both the positive and negative dimensions of life
- Applies mainly phenomenological research methods (studying human life from within).

Humanistic Psychology

- Focuses on human potentialities and virtues
- Emphasises the positive dimensions of life
- Applies mainly phenomenological research methods (studying human life from within).

Positive Psychology

- Focuses on human potentialities and virtues
- Emphasises the positive dimensions of life
- Applies mainly natural science research methods (studying human life from without).

Mainstream Psychology

- Focuses on all aspects of behaviour
- Places a certain emphasis on the negative dimensions of life problems and pathologies
- Applies mainly natural science research methods (studying human life from without).

Together with existential philosophy – its parent discipline – and existential therapy – its main area of application – existential psychology is a truly international accomplishment. The main contributors to the development of existential psychology and its therapeutic application hail from many countries. In Appendix A you will find brief biographies of 23 especially important contributors to this field.

There are a number of books dealing with the fundamentals of existential philosophy. John Macquarrie's *Existentialism* (Macquarrie, 1972) provides an excellent overview. Also, the applied field of existential therapy has been enriched in recent years with quite a number of books. A succinct survey of the therapeutic field has been provided by Mick Cooper in his book *Existential therapies* (Cooper, 2003). For some reason, however, existential psychology, the theoretical and empirical bridge between philosophy and therapy, has been sparsely treated in terms of systematic, coherent expositions. The psychology that was supposed to inform us on how to live our life in the best possible way and how to help our fellow human beings solve their problems in life cannot be found in one single volume. This book is a modest attempt to mend that situation.

CHAPTER 2

HAPPINESS AND SUFFERING

THE CONCEPTS OF HAPPINESS AND SUFFERING

Every human being fosters ideas of happiness and entertains hopes for a happy life. In addition, everybody knows of suffering and wishes to avoid or master this dimension of life. Suffering and happiness belong to the most basic categories of our consciousness. They are often seen as contrasts, a view that we will question later in this chapter.

In behavioural and mainstream psychology, people are said to strive towards pleasure and towards avoiding pain. Such a striving applies to animals and to the animal part of the human being. But a human being is much more than their biology. The most valuable part of any human being is that which distinguishes them from being an animal. Therefore, in humanistic and existential psychology, the biologically oriented concepts of pleasure and pain are expanded to encompass purely psychological and even spiritual experiences; hence the broadened terms of happiness and suffering instead of pleasure and pain.

In everyday language, the term 'happiness' refers to a state or an experience of well-being and contentment. In some cases, it also points to a state of pleasurable satisfaction. Furthermore, in certain contexts the word 'happy' entails the idea of being fortunate.

The term 'suffering' refers to a state or an experience of feeling or enduring pain. The pain may be mental or physical; in milder cases it may appear as discomfort or unpleasantness. It may be associated with defeat, some mishap or a variety of other physical or social conditions.

Happiness and suffering are core psychological states. In what follows, we will elaborate on the content and psychological meaning of these two key concepts.

HAPPINESS IN MAINSTREAM SOCIOLOGY AND PSYCHOLOGY

In recent years, researchers in mainstream sociology and psychology have been endeavouring to measure happiness. Sociologists are particularly devoted to the description of how happiness varies from country to country and across populations, and its relations to various aspects of life and to society in general. Psychologists are particularly interested in pinpointing and describing happiness as a limited, observable psycho-biological state whose characteristics may be outlined with sufficient precision to learn how to bring it about.

A single question often forms the basis of international surveys: *Taking all together, how happy would you say you are (very happy, quite happy, not very happy, not happy at all)?* (Harding, 1986). In other studies, the question is posed as follows: *How satisfied are you with the life you lead (very satisfied, fairly satisfied, not very satisfied, not at all satisfied)?* (Veenhoven, 1993). The questions provide a gauge for life satisfaction or so-called subjective well-being. This measure has turned out to be quite stable and consistent for individuals as well as groups. In the media, this empirical measure for life satisfaction is frequently turned into a benchmark for happiness. However, as we shall see later, happiness is something much more profound.

Recent decades have seen many large-scale, sociologically oriented surveys of the prevalence of subjective well-being or life satisfaction in various countries. According to surveys from the World Values Study Group, Northern European countries time and again show up as the world's leading nations in terms of happiness; while Southern European countries like Spain, Italy, and France appear much further down on the global scale. These research findings appear rather mysterious. Northern Europeans and British nationals who live or stay in Southern European countries often give accounts of how people in these countries know how to appreciate life's pleasures and the art of living. Maybe something similar applies to the relationship between the USA and the Caribbean Islands or Hawaii or Brazil. This is a paradox. Northern Europe and the USA, together with countries such as Canada, Australia and New Zealand, may be said to be good *societies* or *social systems*. However, when one sees how people in other parts of the world talk together on buses and trains and in the streets, sing and dance, rejoice in the enjoyment of a meal, small or large; how they extend their hospitality, express their emotions in a direct and clear manner and sometimes carry themselves with non-aggressive dignity and calmness, one cannot seriously assert that Northern Europe and the USA also hold the world record in joy of life. People here widely display frowns, worries, complaints, bodily tensions and aggressive behaviour in traffic. In his book on happiness, the social psychologist Michael Argyle supports this view: 'These results are hard to believe,' he says (Argyle, 2001, p. 180).

He mentions that some countries simply foster a cultural expectation that people should be satisfied. So when Northern Europeans earn high scores and are placed at the top of the world scale, more than anything this might be a reflection of having been told since childhood that they are blessed with the best opportunities and thus have nothing to complain about, while Italian children have been allowed to voice their feelings of unhappiness with greater intensity.

There exists a corresponding, more psychologically oriented type of research into states of happiness and how to achieve them. Here, too, simplified measurements in the form of questionnaires or rating scales are used with no further explanation of what is really being measured. One consequence of this research is a tendency to equate the psychological state of happiness with certain biological states. Most people feel greater subjective and emotional well-being when the brain emits the calm alpha waves than when the more hectic beta waves are activated. Similarly, a pleasant emotional state occurs when the so-called endorphins flow through the body. Any jogger knows this: At a certain time during running, the organism is flooded by a sudden feeling of lightness and well-being without the person having done anything apart from running. These psycho-biological facts are no doubt highly interesting and relevant. They are not, however, sufficient grounds to equate happiness on the one hand and alpha waves or 'runner's high' on the other. That is biological reductionism. Building on this type of knowledge, some cognitive psychologists and therapists have made lists of happiness-inducing activities, including about 50 items, such as 'being told I am loved', 'having coffee' 'amusing people' 'smiling at people' (Lewinsohn & Graf, 1973). The idea is that if you can make people do some of these things, they will become happier and less depressed. According to this philosophy, the therapists can instruct their clients: 'Look at the list. Do some of these things. Then you will become happier' (Argyle, 2001, pp. 208ff).

In positive psychology, happiness has been studied by Ed Diener, Martin Seligman and others. Positive psychology is a recently developed branch of psychology. Here the positive and constructive dimensions of humankind that we know from humanistic and existential psychology are studied by means of traditional, rigorous and quantitative research methods. From an existential point of view, the achievements of positive psychology are fascinating and impressive. However, there seems to be an unresolved methodological problem in this school in that the subjects studied (e.g. happiness and love) deserve a thorough phenomenological understanding before the questionnaires can be constructed and the statistics computed. Otherwise one runs the risk of not knowing what one is measuring, so the existentialist would say.

Ed Diener's term for happiness is *subjective well-being*. Subjective well-being includes experiencing pleasant emotions, low levels of negative moods and a high degree of life satisfaction. Diener and his colleagues have developed and tested a five-item Satisfaction with Life Scale (Diener *et al.*, 2002, pp. 63ff).

Martin Seligman in his book on authentic happiness argues that it is in fact possible to raise your own level of happiness. He brings together many research findings and applies these results to the general reader in a kind of self-improvement guide to happiness (Seligman, 2002).

Now, in what ways may this sociological and psychological research into life satisfaction or so-called happiness be made useful? Some sociologists believe that you can actually make certain ideological recommendations concerning happiness for politicians to implement. In the UK, the Strategic Office of the Prime Minister has issued recommendations as to how to increase the nation's happiness (Paxton & Dixon, 2004). The cognitively oriented positive psychologists argue that it is in fact possible to programme each other and oneself to experience greater states of happiness.

However, the problem with both these approaches is that they tend to view human beings as mere objects that may be shaped by their surroundings and moulded by political or psycho-educational programmes. There seems to be little room here for a view of the human being as capable of free choice and conscious decision making. This research does not seem to focus on the human being as a person effectuating their *own* goals, values and obligations.

HAPPINESS IN HUMANISTIC PSYCHOLOGY

If it is too narrow to see happiness as a mental state that can be programmed into human beings, or indeed self-programmed, how, then, are we to understand the concept of happiness? We find an attempt towards a broader view in humanistic psychology.

In humanistic psychology, happiness and people's quest for happiness are important themes. A pivotal notion among the humanistic psychologists is that human beings continue to develop throughout their entire life. Charlotte Bühler was one of the many German psychologists who had to immigrate to the USA because of Nazism. While in Germany, she had already conducted surveys of the structure of human lives viewed in their entirety (Bühler, 1959). It was this line of work that she further developed in the USA.

To begin with, Bühler studied whole and completed life circles as they were described in autobiographies and biographies. Examining these lifespans from birth to death, she asked: As a psychologist, how may I understand all these different lives? Through which key concept may I capture the essential core of what I observe here? Right from the outset, Bühler was struck by the fact that the life of any individual, viewed in its entirety, was characterised by inner coherence, by a unifying or integrating principle. She called this integrating principle *intentionality*, a concept she probably adapted from Husserl's philosophy.

Bühler understood intentionality as the life expectations and life tasks that seemed to permeate the lives of the people she studied. Later, as she investigated ordinary people of different ages and gained more experience with clients in therapy, she realised that all human beings apparently have ideas about what they would like to achieve in life. To her, intentionality is the individual's attempt at finding meaning in life. It is to answer the question 'What am I living for?' She subsequently introduced the concept of the *life goal* as an overall term for the way in which humans direct their lives towards something (Bühler & Massarik, 1968).

Charlotte Bühler divided life into five stages, all defined by the individual's relationship to their life goals: (1) the individual develops will, identity and competence to choose; (2) the individual makes preliminary choices about life goals; (3) the individual makes specific and definitive choices of a number of life goals; (4) the individual reviews their life and re-orients themselves regarding the content of the remaining part of life; and (5) the individual rounds off their life and reflects on how good or successful it has been, seen in relation to the individual's own life goals and life values (see also Chapter 3).

Bühler particularly examined the sense of fulfilment of the elderly and their reflection on the life they had lived. Towards the end of their lives, she wrote, people experience unified sensations of fulfilment, of failure, or of an intermediate, mixed state of resignation. Also, people who used to live from one day to the next, later on experience their life as a unity.

According to Bühler, what determines the person's life satisfaction (or, if you will, happiness) is the way he or she *interprets* life. Material conditions and physical and mental recession are less significant, says Bühler: 'Fulfillment seems to result primarily from a constructive and thoughtful way of living; constructive in that even major tragedies and great misfortunes are overcome and used beneficially; thoughtful in that even mediocre potentialities are used for accomplishments and meaningful self-dedication; thoughtful also in the attempt to review and project one's existence and to assess it in whatever terms one believes in' (1968a, pp. 345–346). Your life goals may be clearly formulated or quite vague and implicit, but they still crop up as a theme at the evening of life. Further, if we are psychologists working with clients, they are present as important life factors or central aspects of happiness for all our clients.

Bühler maintains that you become unhappy if you neglect important life goals that you contain. We have probably all met people who in our view lived life in the wrong way in the sense that they had an enormously strong urge for something that, for one reason or the other, they were unable to make happen. It could be to paint pictures or to play music, it could be striving for academic achievement, or it could be to live in a small cottage in the country pursuing a simple, down-to-earth lifestyle.

However, the psychology of Bühler and other humanistic psychologists suffers from certain weaknesses. These weaknesses are also to be found in the thinking of her colleague Abraham Maslow, who from a similar perspective delineates his views on happiness by describing people's self-actualisation and peak experiences (Maslow, 1968, 1970). The major weaknesses in humanistic psychology are firstly a methodological weakness of not being so cogent or rigorous when defining concepts and describing the empirical procedure of the performed studies. Secondly, there is a theoretical weakness in that the humanistic psychologists tend to see the individual as free-floating, detached from the social and cultural context in which they live, isolated from that individual's social world. They are prone to viewing people as consisting of wishes that come from within. If these wishes and goals are not translated into reality, things go awry, or so the humanistic psychologists are inclined to think. This psychology is not so open to the fact that we all have three or four or ten times as many goals as we could possibly effectuate in a lifetime. Many of us have loads of projects that we would gladly undertake if only life gave room for it. We have so many hobbies and interests we might pursue if the world were unlimited. Just imagine all those men or women we might team up with. But existence does have its limits. It also contains accidents and adversity that crop up to some extent in everyone's life. Some people's lives even seem to be literally flooded by mishaps and problems. What these limits and this adversity mean to the question of happiness is not something we hear much about from the joy-oriented and optimistic, humanistic psychologists. But luckily, the existential psychologists can provide us with a more multi-facetted picture of this basic life question.

However, before we can explore the existential concept of happiness we need to delve into the concept of suffering. One difference between the humanistic and the existential view of happiness is in fact that, on the whole, humanistic psychologists tend to disregard the reality of suffering and its importance for their concept of happiness, whereas existential psychologists tend to incorporate suffering in their concept of happiness.

WHAT IS SUFFERING?

Suffering is a state or an experience of pain. The concept of suffering comprises the whole intensity spectrum from mild discomfort to unendurable agony.

The relationship between happiness and suffering is a complex one. From a simple perspective, the two exclude one another. You are happy, or you suffer – this seems to be the kind of thinking common among children and simple minds. However, there *is* no human life without suffering. Therefore, many thinkers have tried to develop a concept of happiness that can incorporate suffering and relate to it in a sustainable way.

In some cases, suffering seems to lead to more rather than less happiness. You find this astonishing reaction in a number of cancer patients. In a thorough study of a heterogeneous group of 33 cancer patients, the researchers put the following question to all the patients:

> Is being diagnosed with cancer an entirely negative experience, or might there also be something positive connected with it?

To the astonishment of the researchers, less than one-third of the patients saw the event as 100 % negative. A little over two-thirds experienced the event as a mixture of something positive and something negative. And more than one in every 10 felt that the positive aspect dominated. Women found it easier than men to see positive aspects in what happened to them (Jacobsen *et al.*, 2000). The following is an example of this type of reaction:

> 'You are forced to review your life', says a 42-year-old female prison warden diagnosed with cancer. 'Instead of running around confused in my life, I started to live in greater harmony. And I have become stronger (…) Because otherwise you start to become a rather lukewarm person, someone who thinks that you have all the possibilities in the world ahead of you if you only have this or that wish fulfilled, and if only so and so happens. All the time you are just in a waiting position. I'm not like that anymore. I'm not waiting for anything. I live every day.'

There are several *areas* of suffering. First there is (1) *physical suffering*, consisting in somatic pain or discomfort. Physical suffering ranges from the bodily pain of people afflicted with serious illness (e.g. cancer patients or traffic accident victims), over the ordinary person's headache or stomach ache, to more diffuse symptoms such as unusual exhaustion, hangovers, or pain caused by exaggerated fitness training. Secondly, we have (2) *mental or psychological suffering* in the form of anxiety, depression, grief, remorse and other painful psychological states. Moreover, regrets in life, excessive ambition, pervasive pessimism or lack of meaning and direction in life all belong to this category. Apart from these two main categories, it makes sense to talk about (3) *social suffering*, in terms of being excluded from social participation, not being recognised, being exposed to racism, xenophobia and other prejudices or being subjected to hostile or aggressive acts, etc.; and (4) *spiritual suffering*, when a person feels pain in relation to the state of our planet or the world as a whole or in relation to the selfishness and deplorable moral attitudes of our time.

Thus as human beings we are susceptible to several areas of suffering. Suffering belongs to our daily life, although many people are disinclined to face up to this fact. What is important for our everyday life quality and life satisfaction is how we *relate* to the unavoidable amount of suffering that permeates our lives in numerous ways.

FOUR WAYS OF DEALING WITH SUFFERING

Human beings have developed various ways of relating to the suffering that emerges in the life of everyone. Also, different cultures have each their way of dealing with suffering.

Some cultures (e.g. the modern Western world) are quite intolerant of suffering and in an artificial way try to eradicate it by means of tranquilisers and other types of medication. The suffering may return, however, in the form of an impoverished and too superficial life quality – a life lacking in depth and rootedness. Some other cultures offer their inhabitants more training in bearing unavoidable suffering with tranquillity and dignity.

Suffering belongs to life. It should of course be diminished and fought whenever possible. But much suffering will still be there. Now, how do we deal with our unavoidable lot of suffering?

The simplest way is of course to complain, that is to project your suffering outwards by crying, screaming or moaning. We find this reaction in children who fall and hurt themselves, but also in adults who are exposed to intense agony or who are not at all used to dealing with suffering. But in the process of growing up, most people develop a more reflective stance towards their suffering. They seem to think: How can I deal with this suffering? How should I face it? Should I focus on it all of the time or should I forget about it? Should I feel self-pity, anger or nothing at all? Should I share it with others?

We may subdivide such reflective stances into four prevalent types: (1) seeing suffering as something to be controlled or mastered; (2) seeing suffering as a phenomenon to enter into a dialogue with; (3) seeing suffering as a positive challenge or gift; and (4) seeing suffering as a fate you can do absolutely nothing about.

In what follows, we will illustrate and discuss these four positions through the example of someone contracting a chronic disease such as cancer, multiple sclerosis or arthritis.

When a human being contracts a disease, they are faced not with one, but with two things to ponder. The first thing is the disease itself with all its medical aspects. The second is the task of developing a *relationship* with their disease. While, from a certain perspective, the disease is the same from one person to the next, the way each individual relates to their disease may vary immensely.

1. Controlling the Disease

First, let us look more closely at the idea that disease is something one may wish to *control*. In recent years, the concept of coping has become a standard term in health literature. The basic idea is that if you are afflicted with illness or pain, the decisive factor is how you handle or manage the situation, the idea of *mastering* or *coping with* the illness.

This idea can be traced back to certain psychologists who interviewed a number of people on how they dealt with profoundly difficult situations in their lives. Based on this, the researchers made a list of the emerging survival strategies and called them 'coping mechanisms' (Kaplan & Patterson, 1993; Sheridan & Radmachter, 1992). According to these studies, coping or mastering mechanisms frequently focus on problem solving and consist of activities such as planning, information gathering, damage control, etc. It may also be directed towards the processing and control of one's feelings by thinking about something else, staying with the feeling in order to 'live it out', daydreaming, repressing one's feelings, burying oneself in other activities and so on. The original idea of the research programme was to study the spontaneously emerging survival or coping mechanisms in humans. Nowadays, however, the concept of coping is often used normatively. It is common to say something like, 'NN is good at coping with her situation.' Some researchers have tried to extract the essence of the coping mechanisms and reformulate it into so-called good advice, which is then offered to the patient.

Yet this research rests on a highly debatable premise: The researchers isolate the 'mechanisms' from the natural human context in which they function. When such strategies are subsequently written down, they will appear as techniques that everybody can use – and human life is turned into a technical matter. If health care professionals then teach patients how to use such techniques, there is a risk that the patients will acquire the same relationship to themselves as they would to an instrument or a tool. Without meaning to, health staff instil into the patients the perception that disease and pain are issues that can be overcome by technical means. But such mastery is not possible with disease and pain, for they are also human realities with a life and logic of their own.

2. Entering into a Dialogue with the Disease

An individual who is afflicted with a disease is faced with the task of finding a way to live with it. They must try to find out if the disease can be made to disappear or if it has come to stay. They have to make friends with the disease or at least get on speaking terms with it. Disease is a *phenomenon*; the individual has to enter into a dialogue with it. Dialogue entails listening. In this context, dialogue is understood as *internal dialogue*; that is, a conversation the individual is having with themselves. One part of the individual speaks to another part, while the other part does the listening; like when you take a stroll in the woods and talk to yourself about how life is going these days.

In the internal dialogue the interlocutor – the partner spoken to – is not an object that can be ordered about, but an entity that is alive and has its own will and logic. If someone wishes to engage in a dialogue with their disease, they have to ask and listen with an open mind, reflect on what the disease has to say to them, explore the demands that the disease has for not making itself too drastically felt, etc.

Jon Kabat-Zinn is a strong advocate of this approach: 'Symptoms of illness and distress, plus your feeling about them, can be viewed as messengers coming to tell you something important about your body or about your mind (…) Killing the messenger and denying the message or raging against it are not intelligent ways of approaching healing. The one thing we don't want to do is to ignore or rupture the essential connections that can complete relevant feedback loops and restore self-regulation and balance. Our real challenge when we have symptoms is to see if we can listen to their messages and really hear them and take them to heart' (Kabat-Zinn, 1990, pp. 280–281).

Pain and suffering cannot be controlled or mastered away. But if the individual can get on speaking terms with them, they will have established the first prerequisite for being able to live with them. According to Medard Boss (Boss, 1994), physical pain is always an injury that concerns the individual's relation to the world as a whole. No kind of physical pain can be understood in isolation, only in terms of what it means for the activities of the whole person. So to understand one's new situation as a patient, one also has to be aware of the consequences for the life situation viewed in its entirety.

Dialogue with the disease also involves the individual's perception of and attitude to the medical diagnosis. Knowing one's own medical diagnosis is generally considered an almost self-evident advantage. Thus, many doctors and psychologists are seriously dedicated to making their patients with chronic diseases accept their diagnosis.

We must ask, however, whether this approach is always fruitful. Who is to say that a human being would not lead a better and happier life without knowing the medical diagnosis? Of course, the diagnosis may provide clarity and security. In the case of diabetes, for instance, knowing the diagnosis may offer obvious health advantages if the patient follows the doctor's advice regarding a revised lifestyle. But, at the same time, the individual must adapt to the role of being ill. They acquire an awareness of the new limits that have now been set for the rest of their life. These limits are partly human in origin and may tend to reduce the life quality of the person, as compared with the life quality of that person prior to the illness.

3. Seeing the Disease as a Gift

Some people are able to embrace their disease as a positive occurrence, an attitude towards disease that to outsiders may seem highly surprising. Consider the following:

A woman in her early 50s diagnosed with breast cancer is asked if she experiences her state of mind differently after having contracted the disease. Her answer is this:

> I feel that I'm only beginning to live now. And that's really true. I wouldn't have been without that disease for anything! And I realised this only six months after I got the diagnosis. That this was a real challenge; that it wasn't all death and destruction. It might result in death, physical death, but until such a time, my opportunities for living could be maximised if I permitted myself to seize them (...) But what's most valuable to me is that I've experienced an enormous freedom. I feel that I have the right to be on this earth. Previously, other people were more important than me. Today I see myself as a pawn in life's game on an equal footing with others; no better, no worse. Just myself with everything I contain. I found out that I had my very own free will to do what I want to do, knowing that I would probably make many mistakes and that this was acceptable too (...) So today, I choose to see my life as one long learning process.

The woman goes on to relate how her body has become more sensitive, and that her experience of both body and soul today bears no resemblance to the way in which she experienced herself prior to the disease:

> Earlier, I saw myself almost like a little robot, running around and being focused in my head all the time, always trying to figure everything out, condemning myself for everything I did and worrying about my future. And the only thing I did not do was focus on the present day. It gives me an incredible freedom; and therefore – when your energy is low – it is also easier to just lie there. Acceptance is the key word, I believe.

This woman has experienced a growing acceptance of herself and she feels really good about that.

Such a statement is by no means unusual. The study from which it derives (Jacobsen *et al.*, 2000) contains a number of similar accounts. The interviewees describe how, prior to their disease, they were very hard on themselves, did not think too highly of themselves and that now, after being afflicted with the disease, they have reached a greater acceptance of themselves and gained access to a whole range of new experiences.

The interviewees say that they have become more alive, more truly present, more open and free; they have improved their relationship with the world in general, have become more themselves and they have come to feel gratitude towards the disease. From an outside point of view, such statements may seem wholly enigmatic. People in good health usually fear serious illness; they find the prospect horrifying and therefore cannot imagine how anyone could possibly attach positive meaning to such a state.

Far from everyone can, in fact, attach positive meaning to disease; it is not implied in what is written here that having the ability to do so is better than not having it! Each human being finds their own solution. But let us consider those people who end up finding something positive in a serious disease that in some cases will lead to their death within a very short time.

Confronted with grave illness, each individual is placed in a situation where they are forced to choose (Spinelli, 1994). The meaning that the individual has hitherto built their life on is suddenly contradicted by the new experience. At this point in time, the individual is compelled to make a very difficult choice: either to accept the new state of affairs and reformulate the meaning of their life, that is change what they live for, or to reject the new state of affairs and cling to the old meaning.

When people are faced with this supremely difficult choice, they sometimes succeed in thoroughly revising the meaning and whole basis of their life. In so doing, they often discover that the meaning previously forming the basis of their lives (e.g. my career is everything; it is all about having a successful family; all about being well behaved, popular, etc.) is now unimportant. It now strikes them as something assimilated from others or inculcated during their childhood, not something they have really embraced as being their own. However undesirable or terrifying it may seem to the ordinary frame of mind, the disease provides an opportunity to choose a meaning and foundation in life that is truly one's own.

4. Experiencing Disease as a Limit Situation

Until now, our examples have been drawn from cases where the individual felt that at least some degree of choice was still possible. But disease can be seemingly insufferable and offer no choice at all. As a side-effect of her medical treatment, a female patient sometimes suffers unbearable pain in her abdomen. She says about the pain:

> When the pain is at its highest, I want to shut out the world and I think: No, I can't contain the world if I have to contain all this as well. But then, when the pain diminishes and is no longer so intense, then I hurry back out into the world (. . .) Some mornings I wake up feeling free from pain, and that's a blessing. And then I can plan what I want to do that day. But if I'm in pain, I can't do anything. Then courage fails me. And this is precisely when it's most important to start cultivating that courage. I need a whole day to summon it up. I believe that you have to have felt something like this on your own body in order to understand

it. I could have done without it. It is so heavy. Then I feel a sense of gratitude entering the scene. I don't know what I feel grateful about, or to whom – maybe to myself, a little: 'Well done, Karen! You are still here.' It's probably because I'm curious. I want to hear more songs; I want to read more books. I want to walk in the woods and do all those things that I've done before, I really would like that. And I have a good view from my window. Remember, from here I can see all the way to the horizon. And I'm really pleased about that. It's also a way of meeting the world. I couldn't live without a view. Nature speaks to me.

This woman has been at the brink of what it is humanly possible to endure. She is forced to live with almost unbearable pain and to accept that fact. But sometimes the pain is gone, and this bestows a particular intensity and sheds a unique light on the life activities that she is subsequently able to unfold.

Box 2.1   Four Ways of Dealing with Disease and Other Types of Suffering

Trying to control the disease/suffering

- trust your cognitive capacity

- see your suffering as a problem to be solved or mastered

- devise solutions and carry them trough.

Entering into a dialogue with the disease/suffering

- listen to what your pain and suffering are telling you

- listen to the way your suffering wants you to live your life

- try to meet the demands of your suffering.

Seeing the disease/suffering as a gift you receive

- focus on what you can learn from the suffering

- focus on the new life dimensions that are opened up

- focus on the new opportunities given and try to be grateful for them.

Acknowledging the disease/suffering as something you cannot change: a limit situation

- at the end: accept that there is something here which you cannot change, whatever you do

- surrender to the fact that there is something bigger than yourself

- accept your suffering as being the life that became yours.

What does it mean to a human being to be forced to the ultimate limit of what is humanly possible, to one's *limit situation?* Karl Jaspers, the German psychiatrist and existential philosopher has formulated a theory concerning this issue, distinguishing between normal situations and limit situations.

A normal situation is one that I can to a certain extent deal with, one that I can compare to other known situations; one that I can influence and co-create; one that I may step in and out of. The limit situation is defined by the fact that it does not change. It is related to our lives in a way which is irrevocable. According to Jaspers, it is like a rock wall we crash into. We cannot change it; only visualise it clearly (Jaspers, 1994, p. 203).

Jaspers mentions facing death and having to tolerate suffering as examples of such limit situations. In these situations, the limit or boundary cannot be moved. Existentially, addressing the limit situation means coming to terms with its specific nature and not trying to avoid this reality by speculating about all sorts of other situations that now will not come to pass. 'The definiteness and specialness of the situation,' says Jaspers, 'become one's *destination* in the realisation of one's existence' (Jaspers, 1994, p. 211). Jaspers pays special attention to the suffering that ensues from being ill. People, he says, will avoid suffering for as long as they possibly can. They will narrow their field of vision; not wanting to know the truth from the doctor; not wanting to acknowledge their disease; not facing the accompanying physical and mental deterioration and not acknowledging their new social position.

One day, however, the suffering will present itself as inevitable. That is the limit situation. Only then, Jaspers says, have I accepted suffering as my lot: I grieve, admit the presence of suffering to myself, live in the tension between acknowledging and not acknowledging, sometimes fighting it, seeking to diminish and postpone it, but *finally I acknowledge that this suffering is mine, it belongs to me. Nobody can take it away again. It becomes my life.* For this state, Jaspers uses the term *amor fati*; that is, you come to love your fate.

Happiness without sorrow, says Jaspers, is emptiness. Initially, suffering may seem to contradict happiness, but – in the long run – 'happiness' without suffering does not make room for living in the deepest sense of the word, real living.

HAPPINESS AS AN EXISTENTIAL CONCEPT

How, then, may we understand happiness from an existential perspective? Happiness evolves in the encounter between the person and the world. It is not enough to see it as a smaller or greater degree of self-realisation, as do many humanistic psychologists. The existential approach seeks to integrate suffering and joy and should be understood as a specific meeting or relationship with the world, a particular way of being-in-the-world.

We have in fact two concepts of happiness: bliss and deep happiness. These two concepts somehow reflect the stance of humanistic and existential psychology respectively. Let us briefly juxtapose the two concepts.

By bliss we understand a state of mind during which the individual feels that all essential needs have been fulfilled and that all essential goals have been reached. The individual feels fulfilled and in some cases even merged with the surroundings or nature itself. Such a state of mind presupposes the exclusion of suffering. Therefore it usually does not last very long. This type of happiness has been described by humanistic psychologists such as Abraham Maslow in his description of people's finest moments, their so-called peak experiences (Maslow, 1968). Later, Mihaly Csikszentmihalyi described similar experiences as 'flow' and developed an interesting theory about how this desirable state may best be obtained and maintained (Csikszentmihalyi, 1992).

Deep happiness can be described as a prolonged state of balance between the individual's wishes, goals and needs on the one hand, and the surroundings or the world on the other. This state is associated with well-being, serenity and relaxation.

Maybe this is the state that the Dalai Lama refers to in his book *The art of happiness: A handbook for living* (Dalai Lama & Cutler, 1998). Here he describes the importance of training your mind in a lifelong process that comprises the moderation of selfish desires, anger, greed, prejudice and negativity and the cultivation of compassion, kindness, humility, respect and love towards other people and all things alive.

We often meet people who can describe their moments of happiness in terms of the first concept of bliss. We rarely meet people who would say that they are happy, basically happy, as in the second concept of deep happiness. Among the existential psychologists, Medard Boss in particular has approached and put into words this existential perspective on happiness. His interest was in understanding the ideal way of being. He developed a truly unique expression for the ideal human being-in-the-world: *composed, joyous serenity* (in German: *heiteres Gelassenheit*).

If we take a closer look at this expression, we may list three components, three basic ideas that constitute it. The first component regards being free, that is, unbound by conventions; you are not a slave, not someone who necessarily has to behave like everyone else or as customs dictate. You may follow your inner voice, your calling. The second component is joy, that is, gaiety, liveliness, vitality. The third component is that there should be serenity, in other words, equanimity, the clarity and the ability to respectfully let the world be (Boss, 1994, p. 112).

It has often been discussed if this composed, joyous serenity should be understood as a state of mind that is quite ordinary, or if we ought to understand it as something completely unique, as an exceptional state. I understand Boss's version of existential happiness as a demanding concept. It describes a state that is rarely encountered. The concept contains many different dimensions. I would like to emphasise these three.

The first one is the *bodily* or *psycho-biological dimension*. Herbert Benson, a physician and stress researcher, has given a name to a particular psycho-biological state during which all the muscles of the body are relaxed, the blood pressure and pulse recede, and inner peace and quiet occur. He calls this wholesome reaction the *relaxation response*: After a physical effort or state of alarm in the organism, the parasympathetic nervous system takes over and brings about bodily and mental peace, quiet and well-being. Such a state regularly occurs during meditation. Body-happiness, one might call it (Benson, 2000). The bodily or psycho-biological dimension is also illustrated in various programmes of meditation and related exercises, for example in Jon Kabat-Zinn work on mindfulness meditation at the Stress Reduction Clinic at the University of Massachusetts Medical Centre (Kabat-Zinn, 1990). In mindfulness meditation you bring your attention to focus on your breath in a quite simple way. This practice leads to experiences of body wholeness and calmness, of feeling at home in your own body, of being yourself. There are other programmes of meditation with a similar effect.

A second dimension of composed, joyous serenity is the *clarity-towards-death dimension*. According to existential thinkers, the most important task that existence poses to each of us is to find out how we wish to relate to the eventual reality of death. Both Gion Condrau and Rollo May have dealt intensively with the nature and basis of death anxiety from an existential angle. Both authors see death anxiety as connected with the degree to which life has been fulfilled or unfulfilled. The idea of 'the unlived life' refers to a person who may physically have completed or gone through his or her life course, but who has not 'really lived', in other words, has not realised their potential and faced the challenges that they have encountered in life. A person who has lived fully and completely will, according to Condrau (1991) and May (1983), experience only a minor degree of death anxiety, whether death comes sooner or later. On the other hand, a person who has found it necessary to give up on many of the challenges that on closer inspection they should have dealt with (be they in the form of activities or relationships) will find it more difficult and painful to take leave of this world. In the words of Martin Heidegger (1926, pp. 318ff), this person has neglected to listen to the calling of their inner conscience. May and Yalom use the expression 'existential guilt' about this state of unlived life; in other words, you owe yourself some life.

The concept of composed, joyous serenity furthermore contains a *spiritual dimension*. The serenity vis-à-vis existence that the concept entails is also a spiritual serenity. The individual has come to terms with and accepts how they feel about their belonging to a greater scheme of things. The greater scheme of things may then be the world order or the planet or the universe or God. This spiritual dimension is discussed further in Chapter 5.

Can we assess how close to or far away from existential happiness a given person is? A single question or two in a questionnaire will certainly not suffice. The final verdict will not appear, I believe, until the moment of death. Not until that moment can we determine if the life of the individual was spent well, based on the conditions that this person was given. The processes involved are difficult to study, not least because the life narrative of the individual may be adjusted and changed right up until the last second.

The processes of approaching life happiness and adjusting one's life accounts are important and active to the very end. For a moving therapeutic example, one may turn to Ernesto Spinelli's case of Elisabeth (Spinelli, 1997, pp. 185ff). There are also a number of outstanding literary descriptions of the moment of death and the end of life. Just think of the violent and terrible death struggle of the old merchant in *Buddenbrooks* by Thomas Mann (Mann, 1994); or the evil and cancer-stricken egotist, Ivan Illich, who in Tolstoy's account suddenly, at the very end of his life, changes and becomes gentle, sensitive and forgiving (Tolstoy, 1976). In his novel *Siddhartha* (Hesse, 1998, p. 199), Hermann Hesse describes a way of dying that presumably existed earlier, but which is rare nowadays: to go out into the woods and simply lie down and die, quietly and serenely:

> Siddhartha bowed low before the departing man. 'I knew it', he said softly. 'Are you going into the woods?' 'Yes, I am going into the woods: I am going into the unity of all things,' said Vasudeva, radiant. And so he went away. Siddhartha watched him, saw his steps full of peace, his face glowing, his form full of light.

For a deeper understanding of this man's journey to death, we might again look to Karl Jaspers. Jaspers describes how human beings think about death all of their lives. Vasudeva of Hesse's novel has thought a lot about death, including his own, and he has achieved a serene relationship to it. Jaspers's view implies that when we are 20 or 30 years of age, we think about death in one way, but when we are 40 or 50, our thinking about death changes. Jaspers has a striking expression for this: 'Death changes with me' (Jaspers, 1994, p. 229). Surely death changed with Vasudeva, culminating in the completely serene relationship to death that the story tells us about; a clear, calm and free relationship of the kind that we also know from Socrates.

Box 2.2   Three Concepts of Happiness

- Happiness is 'subjective well-being'. It consists of pleasant emotions, low levels of negative moods and a high degree of life satisfaction. It can be measured with questionnaires (positive/mainstream psychology)

- Happiness is a deep and lasting state of having realised your basic potential and having lived according to your basic values (humanistic psychology)

- Happiness is your ability to meet the world freely and openly. It is your ability to integrate the joy and the suffering of your life into a long and enduring relationship with the world marked by composed, joyous serenity (existential psychology).

However, this does not just mean that the older you get, the more readily you accept death. Many elderly people find it extremely difficult to leave this world, while some young people can do so with composure and great ease. The latter is an enigma: How come some younger people can leave this world without great problems and with seeming clarity of mind? Here we should listen to Rollo May. Man dies as he has lived, he says. To the extent that you have had the good fortune to live authentically; that is, to do what is basically and profoundly right for you, to that same extent may you eventually leave this world without problems (May, 1983). Medard Boss reasons along the same lines: Why are ordinary people so afraid of dying when this does not seem to be the case with lovers? Ordinary people are afraid to die because they are worried. Lovers live instead of worrying. His theory is that anxiety and love cannot coexist in the same space; so where there is love, anxiety – including death anxiety – is driven out (Boss, 1990). This brings us back to Boss's concept of happiness, the free and limpid tranquillity: composed, joyous serenity. This state comprises clarity and openness in the individual's contact with the world, paired with the will to stand back and let things be. When the existence of the individual is open and free, their mind meets the possibility of its own death with equanimity. Such a mind is attuned to happiness.

THE ROLE OF HAPPINESS IN THERAPY

The concept of happiness ought to be one of the foundational concepts of all psychotherapy. The vast majority of clients are deeply concerned with the problems of happiness and unhappiness. After all, an important reason for seeking therapy is precisely that one does not feel happy. From time to time, even therapists, we hope, reflect on their own happiness or lack of same. But the term happiness is almost absent in most literature on psychotherapy. Why?

Let us take a closer look at the basic interaction taking place whenever a psychologist or other psychotherapist is speaking with a client. The client would like to be happier or at least less unhappy. Indeed, the therapist has their own problems with happiness and their own experiences with happiness. Now, is it the task of the therapist to help the client to become happier?

The answer depends on our concept of happiness and on our view of the therapeutic process. Sigmund Freud considered therapy to be successful if the patient after a completed analysis became able to work and to love. He had hardly any faith in absolute happiness. The majority of Freud's colleagues in the psychoanalytic tradition seem to share a similar conviction that it may be possible to alleviate unhappiness and other kinds of suffering, but that this is not the same as bringing about happiness. Rather, deep suffering is replaced by everyday problems.

The humanistic psychologist Carl Rogers is probably the first to have formulated an ideal therapeutic goal that centres on happiness. He saw the goal as becoming a 'fully functioning person' (Rogers, 1961). The fully functioning person is engaged in a process of change, not characterised by having achieved a certain stable, lasting condition. The therapeutic goal is first of all that the client should become less defensive and more open and receptive in the experience of inner and outer life. Secondly, the client must achieve an increased ability to live in the here and now. What one does in the future grows out of the experience of what one does here and now. Thirdly, one should develop an increased confidence in one's own organism, so that one can increasingly base one's decisions and actions on what immediately feels right.

The existential psychologist Medard Boss states his therapeutic goal as: composed, joyous serenity (Boss, 1994, p. 112). But he also expresses the same idea in a plain phrase: Therapy should enable the client to *meet the world freely and openly*. The words may appear simple, but they point to something of the greatest importance.

The therapist helps the client in this direction through the therapeutic relation itself, which is therefore of the utmost importance in existential therapy. The relation is a caring bond of a specific type. Heidegger states that one may care for another person in two radically different ways. He talks about one kind of care that takes over for the other by *leaping in* for them (*einspringend-beherrschenden*), and another kind of care that *leaps ahead* (*vorspringend-befreienden*). In the care that *leaps in*, the therapist solves the client's problems *for* them. The therapist reduces the client's anxiety and strengthens the client's self-confidence. This is *manipulative care* and it makes the client dependent. In the care that *leaps ahead*, the therapist identifies ways that the client may choose to tread and then stimulates or challenges the client to proceed in that direction. However, the therapist does not take the lead, declaring: This is how you do it. The therapist is able to let the client be and can let the client grow by following their own path. This is *liberating care* (Heidegger, 1926, p. 122).

Here we encounter a delicate balance. The therapist cannot and should not *make* the client 'happy'. If this were possible, it would be tantamount to abuse, as in Heidegger's category of manipulative care. But on the other hand, the therapist should not *not* care about the client's happiness. The therapist should wish for it and contribute to it by having as their main objective to help and stimulate the client to meet the world freely and openly. Let us take a look at these three words. *Meeting* the world – in the words of Martin Buber (1923) – means that the person and the world open up to each other and to each other's being and are enriched by this encounter. *Freely* means that the meeting or the world relation is unshackled; it is a positive, autonomous choice, something that the individual says yes to. *Openly* means giving up your fixed and closed ideas and images of what is out there, relinquishing your ingrained prejudices and being prepared to confront whatever you encounter with an unbiased mind. Openly also means to face the facts of our world, whether they are positive or unpleasant, and to find our feet in relation to them.

The therapist's attitude towards the client is the same as they would have towards a good friend: a commitment to and love of the other person, but also a willingness to let the other person be themselves. To the extent that we can combine a loving commitment to another person with a willingness to let the other person be, to that extent may we help guide the other person towards happiness. The combination of loving interest and the ability to essentially leave the other person in peace – this is the key formula for helping that person to achieve more happiness in life. This is true about the therapeutic relationship and about all other human relationships as well.

CHAPTER 3

LOVE AND ALONENESS

If you ask human beings what really makes life worth living, the most common answer is: *love*. If you ask clients in psychotherapy what it is that they miss or really would like, their answer will often be the same: a life full of love. The significance of love is further emphasised by the fact that people who have been victims, say, of a car accident or have received a fatal diagnosis prioritise the dimension of love more after having been threatened by the perspective of death (Moody, 1989; Ring, 1980).

So, a life full of love is cherished by almost everybody. What, then, is it like to live a loveless life or a life with very little love? Such a life is by many people characterised by the word 'emptiness'. The experience of emptiness is often also felt as aloneness or loneliness. By aloneness we understand the individual's basic recognition of the fact that they are alone in this world, whereas loneliness is the sad emotion that often accompanies this recognition. We consider aloneness to be the more fundamental of the two experiences, even though they are closely related.

Now, you may well ask: Which of the two, *love* or *aloneness*, is the more basic characteristic of human life? And what is the relationship between them?

Some existential authors seem to attribute the most fundamental role to aloneness; that is, to human isolation and loneliness (Moustakas, 1972; Yalom, 1980, pp. 355ff). American writers appear to stress this more than their European counterparts. The Europeans, on the other hand, tend to see love as the primordial of the two. The American existential psychologist Irvin Yalom points out the role of aloneness this way: 'No relationship can eliminate isolation. Each of us is alone in existence. Yet aloneness can be shared in such a way that love compensates for the pain of isolation' (Yalom, 1980, p. 363). The Swiss existential psychiatrist Medard Boss proposes this argument: 'No one can be lonely,' he writes, 'whose being is not ordinarily marked by togetherness with others of his kind. Loneliness always points beyond itself to some coexistence, and human loneliness exists only as privation of man's primary togetherness with others' (Boss, 1994, p. 106). So according to this position, loneliness presupposes a more fundamental state of human coexistence. This difference in American and European outlook might reflect a deeper, general divergence in the way of thinking in the USA and Europe. In his *Of paradise and power: America and Europe in the new world order*, Roger Kagan characterises the American orientation as a 'Hobbesian world of anarchy' with a focus on threats, power and disorder, as opposed to the Europeans' 'Kantian world of perpetual peace', more focused on rules and negotiation (Kagan, 2004, pp. 3, 57).

The relation between love and aloneness is one of opposition. If you are lonely and then experience an abundance of love, your loneliness will tend to diminish or disappear. Some authors hold that love in ample quantities will virtually make loneliness disappear. Erich Fromm, who calls himself a humanistic psychoanalyst – a position very close to the existential one – says that reunion by love is the answer to human separation (Fromm, 1956b, pp. 7ff). Other authors, such as Clark Moustakas, maintain that love does not make loneliness disappear, but gives it a new, richer dimension. 'In the alive person,' he says, 'the rhythms of loneliness and love deepen and enrich human existence. (…) Love has no meaning without loneliness; loneliness becomes real only as a response to love' (Moustakas, 1972, p. 146).

WHAT IS LOVE?

A classical definition of love is: 'a feeling of deep regard, fondness and devotion' (Montagu, 1953, p. 3). But is it possible to describe what love is deep down, its central core? In a certain sense it is impossible to do so rigorously. Love must be lived or experienced. Descriptions of it are best left to the poets. The intense or in other ways strong feelings that characterise love are almost impossible to render in textbook prose. Still, we are going to try.

Let us look at love between two lovers as a prototype of love. A crucial element here is the specific kind of relationship between the two parties, characterised by close or intimate contact, mutual attachment and a strong feeling of belonging together and being connected. The parties have intense, warm, positive feelings that are often experienced as coming from the heart or as being heartfelt in some way. Also, there is a marked tendency for the parties to want to be together and a pronounced feeling of being at home or feeling very good in each other's company.

This relationship now forms the basis for the exchange of symbolic or real gifts: The parties give and receive. They are not just observing one another. They exchange goods actively. One might ask what is more important in this relationship, to give or to receive. Nowadays, people often experience a need for love and care which would seem to indicate love's receptive nature. Still, the giving function must be seen as primary in a love relationship. The feeling of love elicits a need to give to the other, to do good for the other, to be there for the other. To receive the gift of love inspires a desire to reciprocate, to give back. Lovers exchange caresses, flowers, jewellery, food, music, books and many other things, but, first of all, they give and receive their physical and immediate presence. When people grow and come alive by being in a love relationship it has to do with an exchange of a different nature: The lovers mutually see, affirm and acknowledge one another with their love. To be seen, affirmed and acknowledged in one's existence is a basic prerequisite for a person to be able to unfold. By seeing a potential in the other and making it grow, you can bring out something in the other person which they did not know that they contained (Willi, 1997).

Love also entails the ability to let the other person be – what the German Daseins analysts so precisely call *seinlassen*. In being able to let the other person be themselves and be different from me even though I am crazy about them there lies an enormous respect for this other person's autonomy that is perhaps also the acid test of love.

One last pivotal characteristic has been pointed out by the existential philosophers Martin Buber (1983) and Otto Bollnow (1959): Love cannot be planned or commandeered forth. It occurs. I cannot force myself to love someone else if in actual fact I do not. But if I am open and receptive in my world relation, and if I meet others with an open mind, it may happen to me that love for another human being emerges, occurs, overwhelms me. This does not mean to say that there is nothing you can do if love for the other person is waning – there definitely is. But you cannot summon love to come forth on command.

Summing up, the central aspects of love may thus be described as (1) a relationship characterised by a unique connectedness, closeness and sincerity, in which (2) the parties give and receive, that is, exchange symbolic or real gifts, where (3) the relationship is characterised by the ability to let the other person be, and (4) characterised by being a meeting between two people who open themselves to one another as an event that occurs and overwhelms.

VARIOUS TYPES OF LOVE

In the above, we have tried to encapsulate the essence of the phenomenon of love. There are, however, various forms of love. Rollo May points out four kinds of love in the Western tradition: (1) sex (lust, libido); (2) eros (the drive of love to procreate or create, aiming at higher forms of being and relationship); (3) philia (friendship, brotherly love); and (4) agape or caritas (love devoted to the welfare of others) (May, 1972, pp. 37–38). All four types coalesce, May says, in the specific human love experience. In this section, we will discuss the relationship between the first three of these. Agape will be treated in the subsequent section.

Sexual activity is not in itself love, since there is such a thing as loveless sex. In certain cases, the feelings that surface in connection with sexual acts are so powerful that the people involved believe that it is love. But in such cases, these feelings quickly disappear when the act is over.

Love and sex may also fuse in sublime unity. It is difficult to say how common such fusion is. Yet it does exist. In our time it is perhaps more common for a relationship to be characterised by either a strong sexual attraction combined with a certain amount of love; or a high degree of love understood as psychological closeness supplemented with a certain level of sexual attraction. Of course, we also find quite a number of relationships where both psychological closeness and sexual attraction are of low intensity.

In certain cultures and subcultures, sex and love can blend with religious devotion. This trinity is probably close to being the strongest bonding between two people.

Falling in love is not identical with loving or love as we have defined it, but it can be an inductive stage to love, a preliminary phase that later will lead to love; it may also amalgamate with love as erotic love. Perhaps falling in love is a prerequisite for the subsequent development of lasting love. Freud characterised the state of being in love as a kind of neurosis, in which the afflicted person is deluded and in denial of reality, but both Jürg Willi (1997) and Francesco Alberoni (1996) rehabilitate the state of being in love and describe its many positive and developing potentials. 'The only force that is capable of establishing a strong bond outside infancy and outside family ties is *falling in love*,' writes Alberoni (1996, pp. 13–14, original emphasis), and continues: 'Two people with no previous knowledge of each other fall in love and become mutually indispensable, as in a child/parent relationship. This is indeed a truly fascinating phenomenon!' As the reader will know, many marriages suffer from durability problems. One of the reasons could be the absence of a sufficiently intense and obsessive period of being in love prior to the marriage. Nowadays, marriages are often contracted only after the full development of the personality of individuals who are by now very conscious about their own needs and requirements. Therefore, the total merging of the couple is hindered and the basis for a lasting union becomes too thin. The union is eroded before it has become firmly established.

Finally, there is a branch of love that is of the same kind as love, but less intense. This is *friendship* and the feeling of *being fond of*. 'Do you love your spouse?' friends sometimes ask one another. 'Well, that depends on how you define love,' the answer might be, 'but of course I am very fond of him (or her), but more like a friend.' Here we have a weakened love relation that has turned into friendship.

It is important to add that love may also be directed towards objects other than one's fellow human beings. It may be directed towards music, poetry and art; towards nature (the forest, mountains, the sea); towards animals and plants; and towards specific forms of activity such as sport, playing music, etc. It may also be directed towards the world or towards humanity as such, or towards God, in which case it becomes religious love.

IS IT POSSIBLE TO LOVE EVERYBODY?

An important question is this: Can you love only a very limited number of people or is it possible to love mankind or the world as such; in other words, to have a loving attitude to and relationship with everyone you meet? Is universal love possible or not? Should you aim at being generally loving and compassionate towards everybody you come across? Or should you rather reserve your love, care and compassion to the few special people in your life?

We have two contrasting theories with two different answers to this question. They discuss the question under the term *altruism* or *altruistic love*. An altruist (from the Latin *alter*: other) is a person who acts for the other person's sake or for the benefit of the other. This need not imply self-sacrifice. It lies in the concept of altruism that the altruist may have pleasures of their own and may benefit from their altruistic acts (Post, 2002, p. 3).

According to the first of the two theories, the theory of *in-group altruism* or *tribal altruism*, the human being is certainly capable of being altruistic and loving, but only within a defined group (Post, 2002, p. 7). According to this theory, in-group altruism is always accompanied by out-group egoism or out-group hostility. Two of the proponents of this theory, Elliott Sober and David Wilson, claim that the phenomenon of in-group altruism has a strong evolutionary basis because groups compete with other groups all through the evolutionary process. The best group wins. Thus 'group selection favors within-group niceness *and* between-group nastiness' (Sober & Wilson, 1998, p. 9).

The Russian-born sociologist Pitirim A Sorokin worked for many years at Harvard University with studies of love. In one of his studies, he collected 1000 case descriptions of 'American good neighbors' and analysed them in terms of how narrow or wide were the goodness and generosity of the selected persons. He was very impressed by the in-group character of the neighbourly generosity of these people, no matter how genuine and real their helpfulness was. He came to consider it a global problem how to move from this in-group altruism towards a universal altruism (Sorokin, 1954, p. 19).

This leads us to the second of the two theories, the theory of *universal altruism*. The human being, according to this theory, has a fundamental ability to feel and show love towards everybody. Half a century ago, Erich Fromm wrote about universal love under the term 'brotherly love', defined as the responsibility, care, respect and knowledge you bestow on everybody you meet and your wish to further the life prospects of that person. This is the biblical 'love thy neighbour'.

Fromm takes this form to be at the core of all other types of love. Brotherly love, he says, is love for all human beings; it is characterised by its very lack of exclusiveness. Most importantly, if you have developed your capacity for brotherly love, you have developed your capacity for all other types of love (Fromm, 1956b, pp. 47–48).

In a recent exposition, Stephen Post defines this type of altruistic love as 'an intentional affirmation of the other, grounded in biologically given emotional capacities that are elevated by worldview (…) and imitation into the sphere of consistency and abiding loyalty' (Post, 2002, p. 51). According to Post, the concept of altruistic love is closely linked to the concepts of care, compassion, sympathy, benefaction and companionship. There is also a connection to justice.

From time to time, altruistic love may presuppose self-sacrifice and risk-taking. Yet in essence, altruistic love is not sacrifice, but generosity. It is an affective, affirming participation in the being of the other. Altruistic love instils in the recipient joy and a feeling of being at home (Sadler, 1969). The person who receives altruistic love, compassion and care will feel relieved of anxiety and isolation. Generous love as well as its opposites, cruelty and humiliation, seem to have deep and long-lasting effects on all of us.

Although altruistic love is a rather rare phenomenon, the important thing is that it exists at all. It *is* possible to find human beings who transcend the narrowness of narcissistic and very exclusive love and who approach the ideal of altruistic love. From time to time, we meet people who have an overall loving attitude towards their fellow human beings; people who are friendly, encouraging, constructive, warm, charitable, benevolent and generous. Such people can be said to be compassionate. In addition, we meet others who appear to be unkind, condescending, destructive, malevolent, miserly and egocentric, whom we may call unloving.

In one of the few empirical studies dealing with the topic of love from an existential point of view, Prasinos and Tittler (1984) began by accepting the existence of six different styles of human love: (1) eros (passionate), (2) ludus (game-playing), (3) storge (friendship), (4) mania (possessive), (5) agape (selfless), and (6) pragma (logical). One aim of the study was to determine the specific type of love preferred by an individual, but Prasinos and Tittler also asked participants to complete a questionnaire concerning such issues as fear of death and the experience of meaning in life, including more standard psychological questions pertaining to self-esteem and ego strength. One important finding was that agape and mania were at opposite poles from one another, with those participants preferring love styles related to agape scoring higher on parameters called life regard, spirituality, self-esteem and ego strength. Participants who indicated a preference for love styles related to mania scored lowest on these parameters. On the basis of results for each of the other love styles, Prasinos and Tittler concluded that:

> Love style grows out of and is reflective of the larger existential matrix of the individual. Thus, an individual's characteristic approach to intimacy is seen to relate to the other major dimensions of his or her (…) life circumstances. How one loves is part of the larger picture of how one relates to life and to the fact of one's existence (p. 108).

Let me conclude this section on altruistic love by pointing out two major tendencies. The first is an optimistic one: Seen over a span of centuries there seems on the whole to be more and more examples of altruistic love in the world, not least among ordinary people.

The second one is this: People vary widely in their *beliefs* as to whether altruism or egoism is more fundamental to the human being. They seem to hold a strong belief that their own basic assumption is the right one for everyone. They appear to have fundamentally different world views on this point. You will also meet this variation among clients and even among therapists.

Box 3.1   Five Types of Love

Erotic love: A strong, sexually based attraction towards and fascination with another human being, usually of the opposite sex.

Family love: A deep feeling of long-standing attachment, belonging and caring; often found among life partners, parents and children and in other family relations.

Friendship love: A feeling of interest, belonging and caring that often develops in long-lasting friendships.

Universal love: A basic feeling of kindness, caring and compassion directed towards all other human beings. Universal love may be generalised to all living creatures and the ecological state of the globe (also called brotherly love or altruistic love).

Object love: A long-lasting feeling of attachment or affection from a person towards specific animals, objects or activities. Also, love of an ideology and love of one's country belong here.

THE ROLE OF ALONENESS IN HUMAN LIFE

The modern human being often feels alone, socially, physically or mentally, sometimes immersed in a feeling of loneliness fraught with pain. The sense of being alone is particularly prevalent in Western societies and is a result of society's modernisation process. We have three different concepts for being alone, each pointing to a specific state or experience.

Isolation means that a human being is socially alone, encountering sensations such as feeling alone on travels, at work or in the home. Isolation can be thrust on you as well as voluntary, and it may therefore be accompanied by widely differing emotional states. To be isolated is neither inherently good nor bad, it depends on what the person wants.

Loneliness is a feeling of being left to one's own devices and one's own destiny when you would really rather be with others. Feeling lonely is usually negative, often painful, connected with an experience of being abandoned, let down or ostracised against one's own will.

Aloneness signifies the basic recognition that you are alone in the world. The awareness of being alone may emerge in case of illness and death or when travelling in a foreign country. To be alone may be both terrifying and stimulating, depending on the person's natural inclinations and the situational context.

The three concepts – isolation, loneliness, aloneness – thus refer to a social fact, an emotional state and an existential recognition, respectively.

Our experience of the world is always unique, says Ernesto Spinelli (1994). Even though two people observe the same thing, their experience of it will be different because each individual assimilates the experience in its own linguistic, sociocultural and personal world shaped by the individual's life history. But not only is the individual's experience unique, it can never be fully shared with others, says Spinelli, and he continues: 'So you could never fully experience any "thing" as I do, nor could I ever fully experience any "thing" as you do, or as anyone else does. In order to do so, we would have to have complete access to each other's sum total of past and current personal experience. At best, I might make attempts to provide you with some *sense* of my experience of "things", just as you might, but our attempts, though they might be increasingly *adequate*, would never be total or complete' (Spinelli, 1994, pp. 293–294, original emphasis). Each of us is alone in our experience of our world.

When facing death, it is evident that you stand alone. No one can die for someone else, says Irvin Yalom (1980, p. 356). Of course it is possible for somebody to die for me in a war situation or in an accident. But that does not mean that my own death is taken away from me. Nobody can remove my death from me.

We are born alone. We die alone. And in crucial moments, we are often alone, as shown by the following example:

> A female pre-school teacher contracted cancer. She says: 'It quickly became clear to me that it was *my* plight, mine alone. People who haven't experienced it don't know what it's like. I met much kindness, people saying: "Do come over if you need to talk or anything." And "We'd so much like to help you." What with? When I talked to people on the phone, they asked: "How are you?" and I said: "I'm fine", and then we'd talk about everything else. In such moments I've felt very, very, very lonely.'

The interviewee says that she experienced kindness, but she also felt that her surroundings found it difficult to participate in her anxiety and pain. In general, human beings seem to understand each other only if they are in the same situation. To feel profoundly alone, as in the above example, is also to experience that one's life is unique and distinct from the existence of everyone else. I am not just a specimen or a type. I am I. There is no one else like me. This experience of *'mineness'*, of being all one's own, can lead to overwhelming loneliness, but also to a feeling of being something special, irreplaceable, and perhaps therefore to the sense of having a special task or role to fulfil (Macquarrie, 1972, pp. 72–74).

Why is Aloneness so Difficult to Face?

Many people shy away from thoughts like these: I am alone in the world. I will die alone. I was born alone. I will be alone when I bury my loved ones. I differ on important counts from everyone else in this world. Why is realising this so difficult?

One reason may be *fear of standing out socially*. Many people think that they should be like everyone else. Many of us believe that if you are too different from the rest, you risk condemnation and expulsion. This mechanism is particularly strong among young people. Their main concern is often to belong to the group.

> A young man was on holiday in France with a group of other young people. He had looked forward very much to getting away from his daily life because he wanted to try to compose some music. He had brought his guitar and music sheets. He had great expectations.
>
> As it turned out, the project proved to be futile. In order to compose and think in peace, he had to withdraw from the others. But as soon as he did this, he was filled with anxiety, he had to approach the others in the kitchen and common room to be in on what they were doing and to hear what was said about the others. He returned home unfulfilled.

A similar attraction towards the group and away from yourself can be observed in the following example:

> A middle-aged man has recently been divorced. He cannot stand 'to just sit at home', because there he is easily overwhelmed by a feeling of loneliness and abandonment. He has got to get 'out' and hurl himself into hectic social activity, such as touring the pubs or visiting his friends.

In psychoanalytic theory such cases are sometimes explained as instances of separation anxiety, which is believed to have its origins in the small child's separation from the mother. Many psychoanalysts see separation anxiety as the most basic form of anxiety. Existential psychologists recognise separation anxiety, but see it as a derivation of a more fundamental existential anxiety that has to do with living and surviving in the most basic sense.

The thought that you stand alone can be hard to come to terms with. But if you are prepared to face the truth, this realisation may in itself be a turning point, as illustrated by the following example:

> A 46-year-old man, self-employed, mentions his divorce as a situation in which he felt all alone. He lived in an empty house with only a table, a chair and a bed: 'Suddenly I was sitting in this house. It was still as the grave. Everything had been removed. (...) That's what's so shocking. There you are, completely alone with everything. But I have to say: It hardened me so immensely. Because I had sufficient strength to keep myself upright. In fact it made me very hard. And it still influences me. Because I've become more, more – I have got much more power to say: "*That's* how things should be!"'

Secondly, the fear of loneliness may have social and cultural roots. Erich Fromm (1975) points out that man's individuation, the degree to which individuals differ from one other, has increased over the centuries. Today, we are much more individualised and therefore find it much more difficult to stand alone. In contemporary society there are, says Fromm, three mechanisms of escape that the individual may resort to in order to assuage his or her fear of standing alone (Fromm, 1960, Ch 5).

The first one is to throw oneself into an *authoritarian relationship* or symbiosis, to fuse with someone or something outside oneself, be it another person or an organisation. In other words, the individual is driven into the arms of someone or something else so that the two entities merge and enter into mutual dependence.

The second mechanism of escape pointed out by Fromm is *destructiveness*. Destructiveness has traits in common with symbiosis, but is directed towards the actual destruction of someone or something. If I feel powerless and lonely confronted with the world outside, I can destroy it. 'Destructiveness is the outcome of unlived life,' says Fromm (1960, p. 158).

The third mechanism of escape is what Fromm calls *automaton conformity*. The individual ceases to be themselves and instead adopts the kind of personality that is prescribed by the prevailing cultural pattern. The individual becomes like everybody else. In this way, the rift between self and world disappears and with it the fear of being alone. But the price you pay is immense: You lose yourself (Fromm, 1960, p. 160). Fromm explains how not only the person's thoughts, but also their feelings and willpower can be modelled according to the surroundings rather than springing from within.

CAN HUMAN BEINGS LEARN TO STAND ALONE?

How might you develop your ability to stand alone so that you do not have to hide away in symbiosis or in the group? The road goes through accepting the challenges of life. Take a look at this example:

> A woman who was diagnosed with a life-threatening disease describes her process like this: 'It may be the first time in my life that I have really felt that I was very much alone. How to describe it? It was connected with an awful lot of anger and an awful lot of anxiety. And so much helplessness. (...) If I had had a husband who had felt terribly sorry for me and would have done everything to make sure that I felt good, then I wouldn't have been alive at all today, I really don't think so. You see, I would have taken it all in, and I feel certain that I, too, would have felt sorry for me. This way I had my back against the wall, there was only me, and I just had to make the best of it.'

It is as if having your back against the wall in itself elicits the strength. But do we really need to have our backs pressed so firmly against that wall? Nothing prevents a human being from developing the ability to be alone. One example is to be able to feel at home with oneself. Many people need to learn to live on their own; people are not born with that ability. Young adults who have recently left home often flee to hang out in the street or into a relationship instead of working on being present in their own living room and feeling at ease there. And quite a number of people who have married at an early age have never learned how to be alone and do not like to be alone in a house. Many people find it difficult to travel abroad alone, stay in a strange hotel room alone or go for a long walk in the forest alone. But it can all be learned. As Erich Fromm points out, learning to be alone implies 'the growth of self-strength' (1960, p. 23).

Box 3.2   Concepts of Aloneness

Loneliness:	The sad feeling of missing the company of others, of having been abandoned.
Isolation:	The social fact of not having access to the company of others, of being excluded.
Aloneness:	The basic existential recognition of the fact that I am in certain respects alone on this planet.
Individuation 1:	The social and historical development through the past few centuries leading to our contemporary culture where individuals are in fact more estranged from each other than ever before.
Individuation 2:	The personal development through which an individual – according to Jung's psychology – acquires their unique and mature character.

CAN PERSONAL DEVELOPMENT AND SOCIAL BONDS GO HAND IN HAND?

Nowadays, the optimal development of the individual is often in conflict with the social context in which they live. Some people leave their spouse commenting that they have to get away in order to realise their potential. Workplaces, associations and local communities are all familiar with individuals who are uncertain as to whether they want to stay put or to follow an inner drive to go someplace else.

In the following pages, we will explore this perceived incompatibility between the individual and their social bonds. First we will look at what personal development means, next we will examine the nature of social bonds and obligations, and finally we will see how the two can be integrated.

What is Personal Development?

What is at stake when an individual is seized by an insatiable desire to cut loose, realise an inherent capacity for growth and rediscover themselves? Consider these two examples:

A 22-year-old female student living alone in a major city experiences her life situation as painful and difficult. She is doing fine with her studies, at earning money, at living alone and at socialising with friends and with her boyfriend.

But she can't seem to liberate herself from her mother. No matter what she does during the day, no matter what she reads, what clothes she wears, what movies she watches, who she's together with, she is constantly pursued by the thought: What would my mother think about this? It is as if in everything she does she has only two possibilities: Either she has to do like her mother, or else the exact opposite. Her mother has always taken an unusual interest in her daughter and her innermost thoughts and feelings, and she has treated her like a girl-friend. They see each other about once a week and speak on the phone every other day.

The young woman is suffering from insomnia, is loosing weight and is speculating night and day about how to liberate herself from her mother.

A 45-year-old woman with two nearly-grown children and a good marriage has for some years been the manager of a small facility in the social sector. She has felt insecure in connection with her management duties and other work-related tasks. But she is unusually well-liked by her employees, who all see her as an unusually caring and considerate employer, both regarding their social welfare, professional challenges and personal development.

Furthermore, this facility is highly esteemed in the local community, because the employees have solved their tasks very professionally.

Suddenly she's had enough. She now informs her staff that she, too, wants to learn something new. She signs up for a demanding postgraduate course, requiring her to learn new competences. She tells her employees that they will soon be on their own, as she intends to seek new challenges elsewhere. Her language and her way of communicating with others change. Previously she would start every tea or lunch break by inquiring about the others' health and experiences. Now she starts by telling something about her own experiences or some new idea she's had. Her employees are astonished.

What kinds of processes are coming to the fore here? Seemingly, very strong powers are emerging from within. But what is the nature of those powers? What role do they play in the human lifespan? What happens if these powers are unleashed? And what happens if they are suppressed?

The existentially oriented humanistic psychologist Charlotte Bühler has studied these powers and calls them *man's self-determination* (Bühler, 1968a; Bühler & Massarik, 1968). According to Bühler, human beings live intentionally; that is, they are determined by intentions and goals. Bühler sees our *life* goals, what each of us lives for, as so significant that she lets them structure the periods of our life course. There are other theories about the stages of life, for example, Erikson's well-known theory (Erikson, 1959). However, what sets Bühler's theory apart is that it is phenomenological, not theoretically derived. Therefore, it is of special existential interest.

Bühler divides life into five phases with the following approximate age delimitations: (1) the period before the individual determines their life goals, but during which the individual develops will, identity and competence to choose (0–15 years of age); (2) a period with experimenting and preliminary decisions and choices about life goals (15–25 years of age); (3) the individual's decisions concerning life goals become specific and definite (25–45/50 years of age); (4) the individual's assessment of their life as it has been up until now

(45/50–60/65 years of age); (5) a phase of closure during which the individual experiences their life as fulfilled, as a failure or a mixed state of resignation (+60/65 years of age).

Phases 1, 3 and 5 are predominantly stable, while phases 2 and 4 are transitional phases during which new forms of self-determination and self-creation emerge. This is in accordance with the examples above, both of which can be referred to as the two transitional phases.

During the fifth phase, the individual develops awareness about whether the life they have lived has been more or less successful. The most common closure is an end state marked by a certain sense of resignation. Outright despair, or a marked degree of goal fulfilment, is less frequent, but such feelings do exist. People who previously paid almost no attention to the meaning of life little by little begin to do so during this phase, as in the following example (Bühler, 1968b:199):

> Lowell, 62, worked his way up from a very poor beginning to a rather comfortable position and now finds that there is nothing left worth doing. After having reached his goal, he feels empty. Because he has worked so hard, he has lost the ability to enjoy. He has never thought about his life as a whole or about the meaning of life. Unsure about what to do with himself, his whole attitude is permeated by disgust and loathing.

As a rule, Bühler finds, human beings experience all five phases. It is possible, however, for the individual to have some of the phases stretched out over an unusual number of years, while other phases are compressed into a brief period of time. Some reach the later phases when they are advanced in years. Others die young. In case of an accident, a person can of course be torn away prematurely, but others die early with their cycle complete. It is as if they have had an intuition that theirs would be a short life, so that all phases are lived through, only within a shorter time span. Charlotte Bühler mentions the composer Mendelssohn as an example of such a short life in which all the phases found a place.

Taking her point of departure in Charlotte Bühler's analyses, Jolande Jacobi develops and elaborates on the theories of personal development which she, with C.G. Jung, calls individuation. Jacobi was trained by Jung and in her book she discusses his theories. She adds to Bühler's theory the notion that there may be biological as well as spiritual life phases, and that the two levels do not always follow one another (Jacobi, 1983).

Jung's theory on individuation – as expounded by Jolande Jacobi – is relevant to the existential understanding of personal development and is in fact one of the very few comprehensive theories about development in the later phases of life. But Jung is also speculatively oriented and bases his arguments on certain theoretical conditions. A phenomenologist would therefore have to dismantle some of the ideas, but an interesting core remains.

By individuation, Jung understands the gradual realisation of the self as it takes place throughout life. During individuation, the individual develops their completely unique mixture of something universally human and something personal. Each has their inherent possibility for charting their own course, defining their purpose in life. Individuation can therefore make life meaningful for people who feel that they cannot or will not live up to the norms and ideals of the majority. People who have been rejected or despised can rekindle their faith in themselves, regain human dignity and find a role and a place in the world (Samuels, 1985, pp. 101–102). Jung even sees individuated persons as paving the way forward towards more enlightened and civilised cultural states.

Jung sees individuation as a continuous process, a constant journey during which the personality is completed, becomes more whole, finds itself and at the same time realises its potential. It takes courage to stand out from the crowd and individuate, deepen one's personality and find and become oneself. Individuation is a solitary journey (Jacobi, 1983, p. 87).

Individuation is also a struggle in which new voices from the subconscious layers of the psyche call out and fight for their rights, while consciousness, reason and morals take a back seat. The tension between the two can be quite painful, but, according to Jung, the individual will have to wait and not act until the two parties have found one another again. 'Wait, persevere, until a tolerable solution suddenly presents itself, as if it were a third possibility that does justice to both sides,' he says. In this way, the individual is ensured harmony with the unity of the psyche (Jacobi, 1983, pp. 19–20).

Jung distinguishes between two main phases in the individuation process corresponding to the two halves of our life. The first half of life is often dedicated to raising a family, building a career and establishing material security. The second half often has a more cultural aim where the individual glimpses the possibility of death, but acquires the possibility for spiritual growth. The two halves of life are separated by a transitional or mid-life crisis that to Jung marks an important turning point in the individuation process. The first half of life was either extroverted or introverted. Now the neglected part, the one that has lain dormant, wishes to be heard.

The precise age for this turning point varies from individual to individual. If the need for a life change is not respected, says Jung, the result will be neurotic and psychotic breakdowns that are not caused by problems in childhood, but by the fact that the person is currently unable to reorient him or herself (Jacobi, 1983, pp. 42–43).

The individuation process is not just a gradual unfolding of the potentialities of the psyche. It is also a lifelong journey – through living and struggling –

towards the potential wisdom and inner peace of old age. It is a process that 'cannot be grasped in its deepest essence, for it is a part of the mystery of transformation that pervades all creation. It includes the secret of life which is ceaselessly reborn in passing through an ever renewed 'death' (Jacobi, 1983, p. 133).

Now, to what extent are the processes described by Jung and Jacobi common in the real, everyday lives of human beings? Some new-Jungians (Samuels, 1985, pp. 169ff) are quite critical towards Jung's ideas about the development of the adult personality. Why should it, they say, necessarily be a problem to go from the first to the second half of life? Is there any reason to medicalise this point in life and talk about a crisis? Even if many people may become more introverted and pensive in the second half of life, why shouldn't the transition to this stage be smooth and gradual?

From an existential and phenomenological angle, we may take this position vis-à-vis Jung: Jung is correct in reminding us that throughout life, we may experience important personal developments and display new skills that have so far been slumbering and inactive. This can be evolved as a natural process, or it may be encouraged by therapy or other activities. He is also right when he says that in some cases, certain essential life qualities may emerge late in life and the corresponding forces sometimes knock on the door, presenting themselves with great force. This force has been given a strong and poetic expression by German novelist Herman Hesse: 'The bird fights its way out of the egg' (Hesse, 1974, p. 76). Jung is probably also right in saying that if you suppress these forces, a number of diseases may be the undesired outcome.

We do not, however, agree with his assertion that life by necessity falls in two distinct halves, separated by a transition crisis. Nor when he asserts that the second half is necessarily more spiritual than the first. In fact, from a strictly phenomenological perspective it is not possible to impose one single model, one single formula, one single fixed phase division on life. Life is far too multi-facetted and unruly for that and the individuals engaged in existence far too unique. The respect for diversity is central to the phenomenological and existential approach.

Life may very well develop by fits and starts, but it may also proceed in a gradual manner. Some people develop and change dramatically; others are seemingly the same people from birth right until death. For an existentialist, one cannot be said to be better than the other. What is always true is this: *All people contain both realised and unrealised life potentialities. The latter may be unrecognised. Sometimes the unrealised life potentialities emerge with powerful force – they will out. In other cases they just calmly arrive.*

Life is always changing and becoming. Two days are never identical. You are never quite the same on Monday and on Tuesday. Each one of us is always subject to the process of *becoming*, but we may close or open our eyes to this fact.

What are Social Bonds?

A social bond is formed each time humans meet more than once. Before they are aware of it, they have started to relate, create a social bond and become committed.

> A family has just moved to Cambridge. On the pavement the husband meets one of their new neighbours. They start talking, conversing about the weather and about the risk of car thefts in the neighbourhood. A few days later they happen to meet again. This time they talk about the weather, about how well their cars perform and about the football game later that night.
>
> When the two of them meet for the third time, there already exists a social bond. A will greet B; if he didn't, B would be offended. And if B just passes, he would have to signal that he is busy today. Already they have established habits for what they talk about, for how long they talk and how much they reveal of themselves, including which feelings they exhibit or do not exhibit. These habits will be expanded and developed in the time to come.
>
> From now on, the relationship between A and B can never be undone. A will never again be able to *not* know B. The relationship between A and B will exist for the rest of their lives. Whenever they meet, they will know that they know or have known each other (even if they may choose to pretend otherwise). For the rest of their lives A and B will have a relationship.
>
> You can probably say that this relationship, this bond, is formed the *second* time the two persons meet and recognise each other. It exists from then on. You can meet another person briefly one time and then the second time pretend that you do not know each other. (This 'mechanism' may be the reason why one isolated sexual encounter is popular in some circles. Afterwards you can behave as if you don't know each other. The persons concerned want sex, but they don't really want to know each other and to *be* together.)

The phenomenological sociologists Peter L Berger and Thomas Luckmann (Berger & Luckmann, 1991, pp. 74ff) have described the formation of the relationship or bond. The mere fact of two people meeting and interacting marks a beginning institutionalisation. A and B will quickly begin to see recurring patterns and habits in each other. A will begin to expect B to do this or that. Thus a role is formed for B, and B develops their habits. Similarly, B will expect certain acts from A, who thereby establishes their role and habits.

According to Berger and Luckmann, the advantage of developing habits and roles in this way is that the individuals can foresee each others' acts and thereby save time and resources. However, roles and habits often have a fixating and binding effect on the individual. Families, friendships, neighbourhoods, workplaces and associations constitute communities which in turn consist of social bonds. What the people involved do or do not do, what they say or do not say, even what they think and feel or do not think and feel will often be fixed in role patterns, norms and habits. The longer the community or the relationship has lasted, the more fixations; although in principle, all that is social is subject to change. It is the socially compelling nature of habits and roles that makes some people want to break free. The community or the relationship suppresses new forces and skills that the individual is ready to develop.

Can the Personal and the Social Aspects be United?

In marriages as well as in workplaces, there is a continuous challenge: How can I be myself and at the same time be together with the other(s)? Some love relationships oscillate between being together in a close, but suffocating way on the one hand, and being so independent of each other that intimacy and closeness is threatened on the other. Love relationships in general seem to function best when being together and being alone have been developed as two equally important poles in the lives of both individuals.

> A middle-aged, unemployed man 'feels great' when he is on his own. 'I clean the house or spend time in my little workshop or go for a ride on my bike. It doesn't bother me in the least to be alone. I have most days to myself. My wife works in a protected workplace, and when she comes home I make coffee and we sit and talk.'

Can a social relation be both long-standing and really alive at the same time? The solution lies in a distinction between authentic and inauthentic interaction.

The interactions of everyday life are often inauthentic, says John Macquarrie (1972, pp. 118ff). The participants do not involve themselves completely. The interaction does not flow from the self as a whole. Kierkegaard, Nietzsche, Heidegger and Jaspers all, each in their own way, talk about the anonymous mass, the group, the 'they' that the individual follows and adapts to, but in relation to which the individual is not really themselves. The others dominate. The choices, responsibility and character of the individual recede.

Inauthentic interaction suppresses our genuine core of being. It dehumanises and depersonalises. It imposes sameness and shuns everything that departs from the norm.

Authentic interaction, on the other hand, lets the human being emerge in its entirety, freely and responsibly. Only by breaking out of distorted, inauthentic forms of interaction is it possible to genuinely be together. This goes for both groups and individuals that are suppressed. A suppressing relationship must be broken and a sensation of independence and dignity be enjoyed before an affirming and genuine relationship can be built up, says Macquarrie (1972, p. 122).

If a person wishes to belong to long-lasting, committed families, groups and communities and at the same time maintain their aliveness, life feeling and potentials for development, the interaction has to be authentic. If the interaction is inauthentic, it will lead to conflict between the individual and the social surroundings. If the individual wishes to thrive for many years with the same love partner, the same colleagues and the same friends, they will have to exhibit all aspects of themselves in the relationship. Only in this way can the self, the relationship and the other(s) all be in a process of continued becoming.

LOVE AS A CULTURAL AND SOCIAL PHENOMENON

Like all other human phenomena, love takes on a different shape and form of presentation in different cultures and eras. Two questions are particularly pertinent regarding love as a contemporary, cultural phenomenon.

The first question is: What is special about love in its late modern, Western version? A brief answer is this: In late modern, Western societies, love is tied to individuals who live in a fleeting, consumerist, materialistic, self-centred and partly irreligious culture. Our perception of love has sprung from the Romantic period that singles out love as something that is primarily about individuals' feelings for each other. If we go back to the middle ages, we find entirely different perceptions of love. Similarly, the concept of motherly love has undergone significant changes throughout past centuries.

The second question is: Is there, in our time, a specific lack of love? If so, how may we explain this, and how may we be able to mend it? We can approach this question by referring to the work of Erich Fromm.

More than 50 years ago, Erich Fromm presented a profound argument to the effect that a number of individualising, competitive and consumerist structures in our kind of society are enemies of love (Fromm, 1956b). If you observe the typical modern Western individual scurrying down the streets of the cities of the Western world or hear these individuals snarl at each other in traffic, in the workplace and at home, the thought immediately suggests itself: There is a lack of love and warmth here. Here, egotism, greed and coldness are widespread among people. It would, however, take a number of in-depth, comparative anthropological surveys to determine if this impression is correct and if one can rightfully claim that modern Western society lacks love. The relations between power, class structure and love are exceedingly complex in developed as well as less developed countries. In any case, few would differ with the view that the world would be a better place to live in if there was more love and generosity. So it would seem urgent to find out ways in which it might be possible to develop more warmth of heart in our societies.

HELPING CLIENTS WITH PROBLEMS OF LOVE AND ALONENESS

From the above analysis it seems clear that love in our personal and social life is a strongly desirable state. What can we as psychologists and therapists do to help our clients and students lead lives more filled with love?

First of all, we should continue to devote time to the subject of love in our textbooks, journals and conversations among colleagues. In the discipline of psychology as well as related fields such as sociology, philosophy and education there has been a tendency to leave this subject out in the cold and maybe replace it with more mechanistic terms such as 'interpersonal attraction' or 'sexual satisfaction'. Fortunately, several psychologists studying adult development declare that the development of love is a crucial theme. Thus, Erik Erikson sees it as an important challenge in adult life first to approximate the development of generativity as a character trait, then the development of integrity (Erikson, 1959). The way Erikson describes them, both generativity and integrity contain significant love dimensions. Similarly, Jung sees the individuation process as a process during which unrealised life possibilities in the personality emerge and lead to the more spiritually oriented and altruistically oriented form of life that characterises the second half of life (Jacobi, 1983). Charlotte Bühler, too, describes the way human beings reflect on the amount of love in their lives, and how in a mature age they forcefully return to this question and ask themselves if they have lived a good life, and if they have lived the right way as far as love is concerned (Bühler, 1961).

Secondly, giving priority to love is what most people want deep down, but easily forget when caught up in the struggles, stress, consumerism and entertainment of everyday life. One of the fundamental ideas of Irvin Yalom's work is that if you as a therapist (and this applies to teachers, too) can lead the attention of your client (or student) to the basic existential dilemmas that we are all subordinate to, then life's more basic values (such as love) may come to the foreground.

Thirdly, it is important how the therapist or the teacher demonstrates their own world view in their own behaviour. Can the clients or students really feel that this therapist or teacher has their welfare at heart? Does the client or student feel that the therapist or teacher radiates a clear determination that the client or student should feel good and develop positively? Or does the client or student sense the therapist's or teacher's egoism, self-centredness and boastfulness?

Yalom is talking about the therapist's *caritas* (Yalom, 2002). We here arrive at a certain limit for the therapist or teacher, for of course you cannot be or demonstrate something that you are not. The best thing you can do in order not to mystify your surroundings is to show yourself as the person you truly are. But even if the therapist or the teacher at a given point in their own development has a highly developed air of self-centredness and narrow-mindedness, this is by no means the same as saying that this pattern will continue for the rest of their life. There is always the possibility that other patterns will evolve. The therapist or teacher – through their own personal being – always demonstrates to what extent they work to integrate these values of love for fellow human beings. This exemplary impact of the therapist or teacher can hardly be overestimated.

CHAPTER 4

ADVERSITY AND SUCCESS: THE ROLE OF CRISIS IN HUMAN DEVELOPMENT

Human life is a blend of success and adversity. We all experience both of them and we have to work out our personal balance between them. This balance is seriously challenged when external factors intervene in our lives.

What happens to us when we experience a shock coming from the surrounding world: an assault, a traffic accident, a sudden disease, a divorce, the loss of a dear family member or the loss of one's job? What happens when we are thrown into such crisis situations? Why can some of us to transform such situations into vehicles for personal growth while others break down, get stuck and stagnate?

WHAT IS A CRISIS, AND WHAT IS A TRAUMA?

By a psychological crisis we understand a shock to the soul. When a person incurs a psychological crisis, they lose direction, lose their orientation and are profoundly shaken.

The word crisis is also used about bodily, medical afflictions and about economic, social and political turmoil. The word connotes a dangerous situation that is at the same time a turning point or a crossroads involving choice. A society or an organisation enmeshed in crisis is on the brink of breaking down and may develop in widely different directions, depending on what is done about it. The same is true of a human being undergoing a crisis. The concept of crisis may be compared with two related concepts: You maybe struggling with a problem, which is less dramatic than being in a crisis; and you may suffer a breakdown, which is more dramatic.

A crisis and a trauma are two different things. A trauma is a wound or damage to the soul that has been inflicted from the outside. A crisis is the shock to the soul itself. If a trauma is inflicted on somebody, they will often experience a crisis, but a trauma does not necessarily entail a crisis, and a crisis can occur from the inside without a trauma; one may for instance develop a religious or moral crisis.

Existential theorists view crisis as an opening of possibilities. No matter how seriously one is affected, the situation will always contain both pain and possibility. However, the path to possibility goes through pain; the positive is reached by way of the negative.

CRISES AND THERAPY: THREE OTHER SCHOOLS

Apart from the existential approach, there are three major contemporary views of what a crisis is and how it should be dealt with: the catharsis approach, the psychodynamic approach and the post-traumatic stress disorder (PTSD) approach (the latter is often combined with cognitive-behavioural therapy). Each of these three views has its particular strengths, as well as limitations.

Catharsis-oriented bereavement therapy is based on the conviction that grief and crisis are such serious events in the life of the individual that particular effort is needed to bring the grief to expression. Unless this happens, the individual is in danger of becoming fixated in their development. The person affected must come to realise their loss and to vent the attendant feelings of grief. Crying is seen as the central factor in the healing process. The idea is that grief resolution and crying are connected, and that crying heals.

Confrontation and active intervention on the part of the therapist are also emphasised. According to this view, crisis intervention is desirable immediately after a loss. Such intervention may take the form of confronting the grieving person with their privation, so as to release the associated feelings, and of organising the total life situation of the grieving person.

According to an existential and phenomenological approach, however, the therapist cannot know what the other person needs until the client, through calm probing, has opened their mind and thereby given the therapist access to their inner world. Therefore, to demand that the other person immediately confront their loss and redeem their feelings verges on abuse. Such a confrontation runs the risk of violating and breaking down what the other person was supposed to build up: their autonomy.

Psychodynamically oriented crisis therapy is based on psychoanalysis and emphasises the study of the interplay between the acute crisis reaction and the individual's childhood experiences. The basic view here is that if as adults we are subjected to violent abuse, a traffic accident or the sudden loss of a family member, our crisis reaction will often be significantly codetermined by our childhood experiences. From this perspective, the individual's reaction to a trauma nearly always has a pre-history comprising several other traumas that have compounded over an extended period of time. In his own day, Freud regarded so-called war neuroses as reactivations of infantile psychological conflicts. What this approach implies for crisis therapy is that in many cases, treatment will involve extended individual therapy during which the current trauma is understood in the light of childhood trauma.

The existential approach opposes the view that it is childhood experiences that to a significant degree determine the crisis reaction of the adult person. Existential psychologists fully recognise that there is often a thematic relation between violations, the infliction of wounds, transgressions of boundaries and loss of trust in the childhood experiences on the one hand, and the acute crisis experience of the adult on the other. They also recognise that there may be an intricate interplay between the two sets of experiences that should be in the foreground of the therapeutic process. But according to the existential view, the past does not determine the present. On the contrary, the individual's experience of the present and their current self-construct determine what they choose to select from their multi-facetted childhood memories (Spinelli, 1994): a point of view that we will develop further in Chapter 6. Therefore, the therapist should work hands-on with the individual's self-construct and their actual situations of choice in the crisis-resolving process.

The approaches also differ in their view of the optimal duration of the therapy. Many psychodynamically oriented therapists prefer to work over long periods of time towards reaching as complete a resolution of infantile traumas as possible, whereas existential therapists would rather see life as something that always contains difficult dilemmas and tough situations that each one of us has to face. The sooner a person once again embarks on life and lives it using their own resources, the better (van Deurzen-Smith, 1997, p. 249).

The *PTSD-oriented crisis approach* views the crisis as a result of an acute, externally inflicted trauma. Here, the psychological crisis involves a stress load that the individual experiences as overwhelming. The acute reaction is characterised by disruptions of the ability to think, by overwhelming feelings and by reduced behavioural control.

According to this approach, events such as shipwreck, rape, assault, workplace accidents, etc. will result in traumas in most normal people. The individual's childhood history is seen as less relevant. It would of course be best if such traumas could be avoided altogether, but where this is impossible, ways should be found of alleviating them as soon as they occur. Therefore, great importance is attached to extending society's means of handling crises, including timely and efficient intervention for those affected. Therapy is often based on a cognitively inspired version of crisis intervention; that is, dialogue that focuses on the affected person's thought patterns and basic assumptions.

The psychiatric diagnosis PTSD is used as a therapeutic guideline. For this diagnosis to apply, one has to have been exposed to extremely threatening events and to suffer from repeated, invasive recollections of the event, continued avoidance of elements related to the trauma and persistent symptoms of increased levels of activity.

From an existential angle, there is reason to oppose the tendency to medicalise and pathologise normal life. To the existential psychologist, being threatened and robbed in the street, hit by a car or losing a loved one are events that belong within the normal spectrum of human life. It is not a disease. As a human being you must be prepared to get your share of hardship sooner or later. You must develop ways of living that allow you to deal with a little bit of everything. For professionals to label the outcome of a harsh event as a psychiatric disorder verges on pathologising normal, multi-facetted human life. This is not an argument against giving traumatised people access to free or affordable therapy or debriefing with psychologists or other therapists, which is often a wise approach. My point is that such help should not require a prior 'illness' or diagnosis.

Another difference lies in the question of whether or not a crisis can be diagnosed externally by means of objective criteria or whether it should be diagnosed from within as a subjective experience. Using the PTSD diagnosis supports a predominantly external view, even though subjective criteria are also relied on. Yet not only do seemingly identical traumas influence different people in entirely different ways, but more importantly, people's ability to handle or contain a shock to the soul also differs widely. Two people may be equally shaken by an event and marked by PTSD symptoms to a similar degree and yet have vastly different abilities to absorb the trauma, contain it and process it positively. From an existential approach, neither the traumatic event nor the symptoms are of the essence here. What matters is the individual's inner reception of the experience, their ability to contain it and to reflect and act on it.

The prevalent diagnostic systems (ICD-10 and DSM-IV) are viewed with a certain scepticism in existential psychology. Good intentions notwithstanding, to diagnose a fellow human being is also to stigmatise that human being. Once the label has been attached, professionals tend to reduce their openness and sensitivity to the person in question and to their potential. Few psychiatrists, psychologists and psychotherapists like to be diagnosed themselves. They probably sense that being handed a diagnosis easily leads to a shutdown of possibilities for further development.

Each of the three approaches mentioned above has its own merits, but they also share a common weakness: They all view crises as something that should be treated and overcome. They see crisis as an anomaly. They thereby run the risk of pathologising normal human life and of overlooking the self-healing powers that nature has bestowed on our life. This view will be elaborated on below.

THE EXISTENTIAL THEORY OF CRISIS

To be in a crisis is an unusual condition. It is dramatic and extraordinary, but it does belong to normal life. Everybody can expect to experience such a condition once, a few times, or even several times during their lifetime.

Any professional working with other human beings has to be able to recognise a crisis. In what follows, we will describe some of the signs. The core of the matter is that you receive a blow that forces you to your knees. You are on the verge of collapse or of going under, but still have the potential to rebound and flourish again. You have received a shock to your soul, which has been shaken to the core. Important characteristics of this state of this shock are: (1) your structures of space and time (the routines for what you do where and when) have partly broken down; (2) you experience strong and oscillating feelings; and (3) you experience intense mental activity, but your thoughts run in circles or revolve around the same topics instead of engaging in continuous problem solving.

Now, how is such a state experienced from within and what does it look like to outsiders? Below you will find two autobiographical descriptions of a state of crisis; one of a milder sort (although not at all easy) and the other very severe. Both persons later returned to normal life by means of their own resources.

The Immediate Appearance of the Crisis

An elderly woman is asked about the worst situation she has experienced. She answers:

> 'When I was in my 40s I discovered that the man I'd been seeing for some years had met someone a lot younger than me and had been seeing her at the same time as he was seeing me, without my knowing about it.' The woman explains that the feeling of being kept in the dark was the crucial factor here. The woman saw herself as a total failure as a woman and as a human being. She felt she was being ridiculed, that she was no good, that she had been trampled in the dirt; she no longer dared to trust anyone or anything and blacked out completely. She drank herself into a stupor for a couple of days. After a few months, she asked her boyfriend to get out of her life. Later, they met as friends; although for their first few meetings she had to take tranquillisers before seeing him.

Most people experience crises of this intensity at least once during their lives. Some get off more lightly, but not many.

Other people experience crises that clearly express themselves more dramatically. The next example is a female interviewee who lost her son a couple of years prior to the interview:

'It was very, very strange. Suddenly I understood what you sometimes see – headlines in the media – people who throw all their furniture out on the street. I was running around screaming, pulling my hair out. I never sat down, I never lay down, I was just running around. And sometimes I wasn't wearing any clothes. Because why should I be wearing clothes? It didn't matter. And I didn't wash at all. Why wash? It was utterly and completely meaningless. And then there was that which has nearly always saved me: paper and pencil! It was in my living-room, there. I had this thick note-pad. And pencils everywhere. And then I was running back and forth and then I wrote something down on that pad each time I passed it. And then I ran back and forth again. And I wrote and I wrote and I wrote.' (*What did you write?*) 'But I really don't know. Because I've never seen it. But I know where it is. But I'm not sure that I'll ever dare look at it.' (*Were you losing your mind?*) 'Yes. And the only way I could maintain a connection to life was what the pencil happened to write on the paper. It was a kind of reality that was printed there. For what had happened to me wasn't real – yes, it *was* real, but I just couldn't contain it. And I was furious. And I would scream and shout if someone contacted me. They only had to say one wrong word. I was violently furious. They really had to be courageous to come and see me. They couldn't just come and say: 'How are you?' 'I feel like hell!' 'Can't you talk properly?' 'No, I really can't.' 'Well, then we're off again.' 'Fine, get out! And don't you ever come back!' Hell no, they aren't just going to come in here and ask how I am and then just stand there and watch how completely raving mad I am – and look at me. Of course not! They wouldn't be able to stand it. Nor would I. They could leave. Where can *I* go? I can go to some paper. That's the reason I survived. Because no one could stand that. I think I ran around in here for about a fortnight, but I don't really know, because everything, including time, was suspended. I was running around like a wild animal. I can't remember if I got any sleep, but I do remember that someone said that I needed something to make me sleep. And I was absolutely not going to take anything to make me sleep! No chance, because I was afraid that something would be bottled up. And now I was right in the middle of it. And no matter how terrible it was, it was indeed *mine*! And it had to be lived out. I knew that all the way through! That it was necessary. That people might whisper and gossip behind my back, "She's going completely crazy" – I really couldn't care less.'

This woman later became stable and eventually a strong, sensitive and insightful woman who on the one hand has continued to suffer hardship and has had to live with her grief, and on the other has developed a whole plethora of talents, the ability to enjoy small things and an unusual degree of wisdom. Now, let us take a closer look at the processes that take place when a human being is so deeply afflicted.

Bollnow's Theory

Life and crisis belong together. That is the main tenet of the existential philosopher Otto Bollnow (1959). Machines and inorganic matter know nothing of crises, he says. But crises occur in all fields where life is involved.

A crisis, according to Bollnow, is a disruption of the normal course of life. The disruption arises suddenly and with such unusual intensity that life itself seems to be at stake for as long as the crisis lasts. Crises are 'events that due to their critical and dangerous nature stand out from the continuous flow of life in general' (Bollnow, 1966, pp. 9ff). Risk is a crucial element in any crisis: illness may lead to death, a marital crisis to divorce, and a political crisis to war. But the crisis need not necessarily lead to disaster. The experience of living through the crisis may involve the overcoming of danger, experiences of relief and, on a deeper level, a cleansing, the elimination of old issues of conflict and the attainment of a new and higher level of stability.

Bollnow restates the old meaning of the word 'crisis', which can be traced back to Greek and Sanskrit. In these languages, the word has two core meanings: (1) *crisis as cleansing*; the individual must be freed of psychic waste, purified; and (2) *crisis as decision*; the individual must choose between two possibilities; that is, make a decision concerning the direction, the path they are going to take (Bollnow, 1966, p. 34). Bollnow maintains a strict definition of crisis. In his case, the concept is not vulgarised or watered down, as it sometimes tends to be nowadays. For Bollnow, a crisis is something extraordinary and crucial to the person involved.

Crises can occur in different realms of life: health, life values and intellectual activity. For instance, you might suffer a heart attack, you might discover that your marriage or your present work violates your most precious life values, or you might be totally stuck in writing a dissertation or figuring out how to refurbish your home. According to Bollnow, all such crises tend to follow a similar pattern.

In illness, the crisis is a turning point; it may lead in this direction or that. You may die. If you get through the crisis, it may feel as if you have come out through a narrow passage. You draw a sigh of relief and once again breathe freely. Bollnow underscores three traits of the illness crisis which apply to crises in general: (1) the crisis involves a break with the past; (2) the crisis is provoked by external intervention into one's course of development, when it strikes, it has been hurtled at you as if from another sphere; and (3) the old life patterns are dismantled and a new pattern that cannot be derived from the old ones is formed. After the crisis, life begins anew at a different level.

The crisis in life values and life goals exhibits the same structural elements. After a long period of preparation, a human being suddenly realises that they cannot go on living as before. In a liberating moment, they sever certain ties and thereby create an entirely new situation. Crucial elements are: (1) the individual is in a wholly unsupportable and despairing situation, until they develop the willpower to break free; (2) the person's decision about a change entails a clear departure from the former life course (this is a step that cannot be taken by degrees, it has to be taken fully or not at all); and (3) the old life patterns are dismantled and a new pattern is formed at a different level.

Small and large crises occur in the intellectual sphere as well. This happens when a person has to solve a difficult intellectual problem. Intellectual crises are often seen among researchers and artists, but also among students writing their dissertations or among ordinary people. At first, the person is mired in a certain way of seeing the problem or task to be solved. This state of being mired becomes more and more painful. Then suddenly a flash of insight occurs, furnishing you with a wholly new way of seeing the problem; that is, a cognitive restructuring has taken place. Insight cannot be gained step by step, says Bollnow, it comes to you all at once. Something suddenly dawns on you, scales fall from your eyes; it is as if a light is switched on. Frequently in the creative process, the individual will be caught in an impasse of confusion, disorientation and dissatisfaction before the solution suddenly hits you in a fruitful epiphany.

In summary: *A crisis is a sudden disruption of the normal life activity and the continuous flow of life. The crisis is intense and dangerous; it may lead you in one direction or the other. The crisis entails a potential cleansing of the individual and is crucial to their continued momentum of development. The crisis involves a break with the past – a painful and distressing process – and leads to the unfolding of new modes of existence on a level that is different from that of the past.*

From an existential point of view, the most important qualification for the helper in a crisis situation is the *ability to be present*. The crisis-stricken person first of all needs an empathic helper who assists without having projects of their own. It is *co-being* that helps. This means that the helper, being open and alert, is focused on containing and receiving whatever comes up. An important prerequisite for this is that the helper has personally experienced and got to know life; that the helper has confronted the basic facts of their own existence.

THE THREE DIMENSIONS OF A CRISIS

Every crisis has three dimensions: loss, adversity and what we may call an opening-of-existence. The individual plunged into crisis loses something. They face adversity. Yet they also have the opportunity to let their life take root on a deeper level than before. Let us look more closely at these three dimensions.

Crisis as Loss

Crisis involves loss. The individual loses something that they subsequently miss. The reaction to this loss is grief. Through grieving, one comes to terms with deprivation, in so far as this is possible. In this process, the joy of life is gradually restored. A serious crisis often involves four kinds of loss. For professionals that help other people through their crises, it is crucial to be aware of all these types of loss, so that they can all be dealt with in the helping process.

1. There are *physical losses*, such as when a person loses someone close, his house burns down, or the individual is forced to leave her home country. The loss might also be a part of one's body as a result of an accident or surgery, for example a leg or a breast or an eye. The loss is of course not only a specific object or person or part of the body, but a vast array of functions, relations and emotions that were attached to that object. In spite of this and the deep pain that follows, such direct and specific losses do have the advantage of being clearly recognisable.

2. The loss is less specific if it is a *psychological loss*, such as a mental change in a family member. This may happen if one of your family members or close friends develops certain types of illness (such as Alzheimer's or a psychotic condition) or if the person develops wholly new characteristics, values or manners; say, through religious conversion or the like. In these cases, the body of the other person remains intact, but the connection to their mind or soul as one knew it is lost.

A person who gets a new job, moves to a new country or who changes political or religious affiliation might also experience various psychological losses in relation to the old and now abandoned job, country or ideological anchorage. These losses may be certain forms of social interaction, certain moods, certain feelings of togetherness and ways of communicating. This can lead to vague or even oppressive feelings of privation that can be very difficult to deal with.

According to the American psychologist John Schneider, a person's losses should be resolved in all their aspects: emotionally, bodily, behaviourally and spiritually (Schneider, 1984). Schneider states that nearly all people carry around many losses that may cause them to stagnate – losses that the person may process individually, together with friends or in a professional context. Schneider's aspects are no doubt important to keep in mind. However, it is possible that Schneider exaggerates the role of loss in the development of the personality. At the end of the day, life itself is one long series of losses, and still it is lived, sometimes even with no small amount of joy.

3. A third kind of loss seen in all crises of a certain intensity is the individual's *loss of meaning and world view*. The American psychologist Ronnie Janoff-Bulman has paid particular attention to this aspect. She works with the psychological effects of traumas resulting from rape, incest, accidents, natural disasters and life-threatening illness. An important effect of such events is that they disrupt the individual's basic assumptions about the world. According to Janoff-Bulman, most people build their lives on three basic assumptions: (1) the world is basically benevolent (as a general rule, other people will be positively or neutrally inclined towards me); (2) the world is meaningful and predictable (the one who behaves reasonably will in turn be treated reasonably); and (3) I am worthy (i.e. sufficiently good, competent and decent). In sum, the basic expectation of most people is that 'we are good people who live in a benevolent, meaningful world' (Janoff-Bulman, 1992, p. 12). If such a person is suddenly exposed to a hold-up or an act of terrorism or is assaulted in the street or raped, their basic expectations in life and of the world are disrupted. You lose your faith in the world, so to speak, and find it difficult to conclude what you should think and believe, what basic expectations you can allow yourself to harbour. Is it at all possible to trust anyone anymore? An important point made by Janoff-Bulman is that a traumatised person will often have their world view shaken and that, usually, building up a new one will be fraught with great difficulty.

4. A fourth type of loss is especially accentuated by existential thinkers: the individual that is hit by a crisis loses part of the unfolding of their own life and hence *part of themselves*. These are the *existential losses*. Experiencing a rupture in relation to someone close to you or losing a cherished object disposes the mind to grief, says Medard Boss. 'Gone is the possibility of ever again being with and at that object (...) the human existence is in fact ruptured and broken in a certain sense' (Boss, 1994, p. 114).

Boss continues: 'When something escapes me, my relationship to that thing is also lost, and these relationships to what is present in my existential openness are just what make up my existence and make me what I am. To the extent to which presences escape me and I forget them, I am diminished as a human existence' (Boss, 1994, p. 118).

Thus, when you lose another person or some cherished object, you also lose the relationship to that other person or thing. You lose the part of yourself that was attached to the other person or thing. Further, you lose the particular fullness of life that was associated with that relationship.

Otto Bollnow says something similar in connection with the death of a spouse or a close friend. In loving co-existence you create space for one another and build a common space. If the other person dies, that common space is destroyed. The bereaved does not inhabit their world in the same way as before. Therefore, the death of a loved one is also a loss of one's own existence. The bereaved individual is diminished. The death of a loved one is a piece of one's own death.

However, the pattern is different with less crucial losses. In these cases, the consequences might be the need to make a laborious new start or a notable reduction in life's opportunities. But, says Bollnow, something within the person remains, something that is not affected by these deprivations. On the contrary, that something emerges as a spark of resolution once you are confronted with such deprivation.

Thus, Bollnow distinguishes between core losses that affect us in our very existence, and less pivotal losses that make what remains more apparent. Boss, on the other hand, seems to hold that all significant losses are tantamount to a reduction of existence; everything that a human being loses contact with entails reduction. This could be construed to mean that people are continuously reduced throughout life. But Boss's approach should be compared with his basic view of humans as beings that are open and receiving, and to whom new phenomena continue to emerge in the field of awareness. According to Boss, human beings are able to accommodate these recurrent losses, yet still grow and be vital and active, precisely because of their basic openness to the world.

So the two theories diverge somewhat concerning the relation between your loss and your existence. According to Bollnow, less crucial losses do not hit you in your central core of existence; new initiatives will emerge from this core to restore the situation. Conversely, the most crucial losses do assail you in that core and make you shrink until part of you dies. According to Boss, all losses make you shrink and obliterate important values from your existence; but only for a while. Because you are an open and receptive being, new phenomena may enter your world, replenish it and revitalise your being in the world.

Crisis as Adversity

Many of us do not find life on this earth easy, and some of us are hit dispro-portionately hard. Illness, accidents and deaths may rain down on the same person in rapid succession. Jean-Paul Sartre uses the term 'coefficient of adver-sity' to signify the amount of affliction that nature, destiny or chance seems to have in store for each of us (Sartre, 1969, pp. 324, 629). Adversity seems to be unevenly distributed. Nature has endowed some of us with peculiar looks that make it difficult for us to find a partner to love or to find a job. Some have a physical disability that creates distance. Others are hit by painful illnesses that make them depressed and partially unfit for work. And still others grow up under conditions that result in serious psychological problems or lead to failure in terms of getting proper schooling and education.

You cannot change such given conditions. But there is still one essential option: you may decide how you wish to *tackle* your disabilities, illnesses, shortcomings or adversity in general. Do you choose to be embittered, angry or depressed and thereby reinforce your initial coefficient of adversity? Or do you choose to apply your strength in this struggle and seek solutions and satisfactions wherever possible? Thoughts like 'I'm ugly', 'I'm stupid', 'I can't find work' or 'people don't want to be with someone like me' all enhance adversity and failure, as opposed to thoughts like 'I'll think of something', 'they won't get me down', or 'we all have a right to be here'. Individuals cannot choose how strong, healthy, beautiful or talented they are, nor can they choose their parents. However, they *can* influence the way they wish to react towards and live with the conditions they have been given.

What is given is our destiny. We must accept it or come to terms with it. Each of us was born as a man or a woman, with a certain height, with blue-grey or with brown eyes, with or without freckles. Our body has a certain shape. We may have been born with a particular illness. We may have been beaten up as children, or have had a mother who was an alcoholic. All such things are destiny. You cannot change such facts. You must accept them as your basis, your existential ground. If you do not accept them, you will be living on false pretences. You will shut yourself off from your own ground.

Several existential thinkers use the word *facticity* to describe what is given for each one of us. The specifics of my destiny or facticity have not been chosen by me. For one thing, I did not ask to be born. No one chooses to come into this world. Suddenly I am in the midst of things. The fact that I am here is a brutal, inexplicable one. I do not know where I come from. The only thing I know for certain is that I exist.

Each human being has their own facticity. I cannot live someone else's life, and no one else can live mine. Martin Heidegger invented the term *thrownness* to describe this state. We are all thrown into existence, and each of us is thrown into their own existential situation. You may picture your allotted destiny as a kind of cast of the dice: each of us comes away from the shake with a particular race, nationality, economic background, temperament, appearance, gender and intelligence.

To exist is in effect to immerse oneself fully in one's actual situation. The answer to the adversity of life is thus to accept one's facticity and to act on that basis.

Crisis as Opening of Existence

A crisis provides the option of opening up to the depths of existence. When someone is thrown into a crisis, it is as if a crevice opens in the ground that was previously covered with sand, in much the same way as crevices appear in the earth during an earthquake. The crevice allows the individual to look deep into something very significant. In this way, the crisis becomes existential and can become a personal turning point, a new life possibility. What is it, then, that the crisis-stricken person gets a chance to peer into?

Due to all the disruption, the individual gets an opportunity to look at what life is really about. We can compare this to the opportunity the geologist gets when a volcano erupts: Everything shakes and melts, but the geologist gets a unique chance to see what is actually down there.

Take for instance a man involved in a train crash. He is severely wounded and almost killed. He is shocked and suddenly realises that what he has taken for granted is not so certain after all. Life is not as self-evident as he thought it would be. He could have died without warning in five seconds, with no time to say goodbye to his loved ones. The fundamental conditions of existence suddenly reveal themselves in all their nakedness. The covers are torn away from everyday life.

What, then, is the abyss that the crisis-stricken individual gets a unique chance to gaze into and find their own two feet in relation to? It is precisely our fundamental conditions of existence. As mentioned in Chapter 1, Irvin D Yalom enumerates four basic existential concerns: (1) death (we live now, but one day we are going to die); (2) freedom (we structure our lives ourselves, but out of emptiness); (3) isolation (we are born and die alone, but we need other people and a sense of community); and (4) meaninglessness (we seek and construct life meaning, but in a universe without meaning) (Yalom, 1980).

Now, according to Yalom, to be struck by a crisis is a disruptive, but also fertile opportunity to find one's position in relation to these four basic existential dilemmas. This assertion of Yalom's was empirically explored in a study of the *Scandinavian Star* shipwreck in 1990. On its way from Norway to Denmark, the *Scandinavian Star* caught fire, resulting in 159 casualties. On board were many families on holiday. The survivors were later interviewed by Danish psychologists. The interviews placed particular emphasis on whether the crisis reaction of the survivors had heightened their awareness towards Yalom's four basic existential concerns. A large number of participants in the study had in fact become more aware of and in contact with the four basic existential dimensions (Elklit *et al.*, 1995).

According to Otto Bollnow, crises belong to human nature as painful, but important ways to development. Inspired by Søren Kierkegaard, Bollnow formulates his view poignantly: Human life, he says, is not just there. It has to be taken over. This taking over your own life does not occur in everyday situations, but in extraordinary situations (Bollnow, 1966, pp. 12–13, pp. 39ff). In moments of crisis, life is lived with particular intensity. Thus, according to Bollnow, crisis has a vital role to play in life. It is through crisis that a human being rises from a need-driven everyday life to a conscious and authentic life.

HOW DO I GET THROUGH A CRISIS?

When a person is hit by a crisis, many important processes have to be taken care of. This applies whether or not the person takes care of themselves; whether or not friends or family members look after the person; whether or not a therapist or another professional helps the person through the crisis. In any event, the goal is *not* to *overcome* or surmount the crisis as if it were a disease. The goal is to *live through the crisis* in an open and constructive way and to learn something for the future. Living through the crisis involves three important aspects that we will discuss in the following section.

You Have to Let Feelings and Moods Emerge and to Sense and Express Them

A crisis usually gives rise to strong and varied feelings, not only in the moment when it occurs, but often for a long time afterwards as well. Grief, anger, guilt, shame, despair, anxiety and other feelings surface, lodge in the body, shape one's thoughts and mark one's actions. Often people get quite scared by the feelings that emerge within them.

It is important to discover these feelings, sense them and become aware of them. You have to get to know them; you have to accept and acknowledge them. It is necessary to realise that these feelings are part of yourself. What matters is to get on speaking terms with them, to establish an inner dialogue with them.

The expression of feelings may take many forms. For some, the most natural thing is to yell them out. For others, a quiet tear in a peaceful and contemplative moment will be the right thing. There are no hard-and-fast rules for this sort of thing; each person has their distinctive way of sensing, living out and expressing feelings.

Some people argue that feelings have to be released. But that is not a fortunate expression. Feelings should not be driven out of the body. They should stay in there. They belong to the individual. One needs to be able to contain them, give shelter to them, live with them, make them one's own.

In her book, *Existential counselling and psychotherapy in practice*, Emmy van Deurzen provides an overview of the most common feelings (van Deurzen, 2002). She arranges these feelings in a circle and regards them as succeeding one another in a cycle that consists in losing something you love and gaining something valuable instead. The feelings are: pride, jealousy, anger, fear and sorrow along the loss dimension, and guilt, desire, hope, love and joy along the gain dimension. Each of these has a destructive and a constructive side, and van Deurzen emphasises that it is not the vociferous expression of these feelings that counts. What is important is to understand what the feeling reveals about the way one is currently living and the way one might live in the future.

Recognising your inner multitude of feelings is a way of reconnecting to the world and feeling at home in the world once again. Van Deurzen emphasises the need for a person to experience the many different feelings that well up, to learn how to feel at home with them and learn something from them about one's way of life – as it was, is and will be.

You Must Try to Reintegrate Split-off Material so that the Self is Healed

When you are subjected to a brutal or horrifying traumatic episode, your openness to the world cannot be maintained. Your defences are mobilised and you withdraw into your shell like a tortoise. The muscles may become extremely tense in the exertion to cope. Some of the things that are experienced are so terrible that consciousness cannot contain them. This is typically true in the case of attacks, terror, rape, hold-ups, traffic accidents, disasters, torture and the very difficult circumstances in which kindness and repulsiveness merge, as in incest and violence in the home.

When enmeshed in such a predicament, a multitude of elements race through the victim's head in a chaotic pattern: threats, blows, bodily pain, thoughts, feelings and observations. Much of this cannot be absorbed by the open awareness and has to be expelled. Later, it will not be readily accessible. Step by step, the individual has to recover the details: What happened? What did the surroundings look like? Who said what? What went through my mind? Common experience shows that it is important to tell one's story over and over again; and the greater the detail, the better.

What is actually involved in this well-known process? Why can't the experiences be assimilated to begin with? And why must they be nurtured back to light? Psychoanalytic psychology explains this by saying that the experiences are repressed and are therefore relegated to the unconscious. Later, the repressed material has to be recovered. Existential psychologists and therapists are often sceptical towards the concepts of repression and the unconscious, which they feel entail unnecessarily going behind the back of the individual in question.

Ernesto Spinelli explains the phenomena described above through a theory of dissociated, or divided, consciousness (Spinelli, 1994, pp. 152ff). Certain aspects of the traumatic experience will be placed in one compartment of consciousness, other aspects in a different compartment. Perhaps the most humiliating and anxiety-ridden experiences are placed in the first compartment (which is currently not remembered, but vaguely sensed nonetheless); while the memories of how the individual tried to do something, such as fight back or help others, end up in the second compartment and are readily remembered. But why is the material sorted in this way?

According to Spinelli, this happens because the individual's self-construct is placed in the second compartment. The self is one of the most precious aspects of the individual. It contains the individual's deeply rooted and often hard-earned belief in what kind of person they are.

When a traumatic event occurs, the individual will usually behave in a way that seriously conflicts with their fundamental belief in who they are, and what they stand for. The memories of this self-threatening behaviour, say, that the individual did not dare to speak up and did not help his bleeding neighbour are split off because they cannot be tolerated under the same roof as the self.

Therefore, an important part of the repair process consists in the individual's exploration and confrontation of their beliefs and assumptions about what kind of person they are. Do they really believe that all that matters is to be respectable, or helpful, bright, brave or perfect?

Such deeply held assumptions, for example that you always have to be respectable or perfect, will block a person not only from the memories that were rejected during the particular event, but also from generally being able to encounter important aspects of the world openly.

Crisis resolution may thus lead from a disgusting and terrible experience to a new insight and opening of the self, to a dialogue with one's basic assumptions about the world and eventually to actual self-development.

You Should Embrace this Unique Chance to Reconsider the Meaning and Direction of Your Life

The spontaneous reaction to a traumatic crisis is often 'how meaningless this is, how utterly meaningless that he should die, that she of all people should fall ill, that precisely that child should suffer.' A person who is suffering a serious loss or trauma will often be seized by a pervasive feeling of meaninglessness that can persist for a long time.

Any helper should always respect the other person's feeling of meaninglessness and continue just to be present for them. If this is achieved, sooner or later life's own forces will usually reassert themselves in an effort to construct a new meaning in life (Jacobsen, 1997):

> In a therapy group, several members simultaneously experienced the death of someone close to them. The grief of one member replaced that of the other, and the group members shared in each other's losses. One day, one of the group members came up with the sentence: 'He shall not have lived in vain.' This sentence became a shared way of dealing with the losses. Because of the death of a young family member, a young woman changed the direction of her career in order to be able to work with the problems associated with the illness that caused the death. A middle-aged woman consciously decided to carry on some of the values that her recently deceased father had stood for.

A survey of the existential problems of cancer patients has shown that a number of patients come to see their cancer as something positive (Jacobsen *et al.*, 2000). Immediately after receiving the diagnosis they are, like everyone else, horrified, but at some stage, the situation changes. This phenomenon is called positive reconstruction. It is quite mysterious what type of mental functions we are dealing with here, and why the reconstruction occurs for some people and not for others. Here are some examples of positive reconstruction from the study:

> 'The cancer told me that I had more to learn. I had to learn to forgive – and to feel the forgiveness within me. I hadn't learned enough from my bouts with depression' (female breast cancer patient, 56 years old).

> 'You get a different perspective on life. I don't have time to sulk' (24-year-old male nursery school teacher with cancer of the testicles).

> 'Most of the time I believe that this is meaningful (...) The meaning is this: internal growth. I have managed to go against the norms and ideas about how one "should" be (...) I will be able to live more honestly and sincerely' (former nurse, 45 years of age, with cancer of the bone marrow).

The meaning that the individual might discern in their illness is often deeply personal and may be a reminder or a warning that it is now or never if they are going to change their life. They may begin to see the illness as something that was necessary, though unfortunate, in order to discover, learn or become aware of certain things.

Box 4.1   Existential Crisis Therapy

Things to remember when helping somebody (or yourself) through a crisis:

- Has the person confronted and articulated all the losses implied in the crisis situation (physical losses, psychological losses, world view losses, existential losses)?

- Has the person seized the opportunity to accept what is given to them, their facticity, as their (new) ground of existence?

- Has the person made use of the opportunity to confront themselves with the basic existential conditions and develop a firmer rooting in relation to these conditions?

- Has the person had the chance to sense, recognise and express all the feelings that the crisis has elicited?

- Has the person had the chance to confront the material that was split off during the traumatic event and to reconsider their basic beliefs and assumptions about themselves?

- Has the person tried to find some meaning in the traumatic event and to draw consequences for the goals and direction of their future life?

The reconstructed meaning and orientation of one's life is for some people characterised by a more intense and intimate life that contains elements of forgiveness and reconciliation, acceptance and coming to terms with existence.

Other people realise aspects of themselves that have previously slumbered, abilities that have hitherto been unable to flourish, such as creative and artistic talents or the enjoyment of nature.

Still others make new world attachments. They become more active in society, perhaps in grassroots movements or educational work; they often wish to pass on their experience and insight to society and the world.

Thus the reconstructed meaning and orientation of one's life may be captured in phrases such as: Through the crisis you find yourself and you even become more truly yourself.

ARE CRISES DESIRABLE OR UNDESIRABLE?

Crises hurt. Should they for that reason be avoided as far as possible? Should we aim at a crisis-free life? There is no simple answer.

A crisis should not be passively endured, says Bollnow in his book on crisis and new beginning (1966). It should lead to *criticism* (the two words both originate in the Greek word *krinein*, meaning to separate, decide, cleanse). Criticism involves taking a stand towards reality. It involves taking an independent look at the course of events and asserting the validity of people's statements. In criticism, true is separated from false, genuine from fake. Through criticism, the individual raises themselves above the mass and become a free, responsible individual.

However, according to Bollnow it is not possible for a person to become critical of their own most treasured convictions using their own strengths. To that end, the individual needs to be shaken by outside events. Profound criticism does not evolve from a smooth developmental process.

Therefore, the development of critical world citizens presupposes the occurrence of crises in the life and development of each individual. It is paramount today that the individual possesses critical awareness towards what happens in the world. This critical awareness can only be gained through crisis. Crisis and criticism therefore belong together and presuppose one another.

Today, in the richest part of the world, a life free of suffering and crisis seems to be within everybody's reach. But will such a life have any kind of depth? Will people be able to feel that they live at all? Won't the result be a society in which the individual is indistinguishable from the mass?

Crisis is painful, but it is also a chance to really sense the world, to feel it. It is a chance to find yourself, clarify your values and take over your own life.

CHAPTER 5

DEATH ANXIETY AND LIFE COMMITMENT

Every human being knows it: one day I am going to die. Many of us do not want to entertain this thought, but if we cannot face that part of reality, we will also find difficulty answering the question: Am I making the proper use of my life? Will I – when that day comes – be able to look back on my life and say to myself: Yes, I used my talents and gifts the way I should have done, and I acted in the way I should have done in relation to other people.

So we have to help ourselves and each other to get accustomed to the thought of death and to face the consequences for the way we live.

Death has become a taboo to modern human beings. In earlier days, dramatic death struggles were part of everyday life. Thomas Mann and Leo Tolstoy both describe the violent deathbed scenes of times gone by (Mann, 1994; Tolstoy, 1976). Today, the health sector has eradicated the death struggle from our culture by means of morphine. People say about a newly deceased person: They passed away peacefully. They value the idea that death occurred without the person feeling it or suffering from it. But why has it become tabooed to feel the onset of death? Do we shy away from knowing that it is precisely now, at this very moment, that we are going to leave this world? People in hospitals are sometimes kept physically alive almost regardless of their condition. Citizens well into their 80s are sometimes referred for treatment whether or not their natural life-flow has ebbed away. It is as if they *must* be kept alive at all costs.

Considering this fighting spirit of the health services, it is thought-provoking that so many people choose to die by their own hand. Nobody knows what to do with all these suicides. Might they be some kind of message to society that quality of life is more important than length of life?

Death anxiety has a special relation to life commitment that can be described as a basic dilemma of human life: If you are too frightened of death you cannot be properly fulfilled in your life. Death anxiety gives you life anxiety. But if you can meet death openly, look death squarely in the eye, then your energies, powers and life courage are set free. You can fully focus on solving the tasks and enjoying the pleasures of this life; in other words, be fully committed to life.

In this chapter we will deal with the process of dying and the theories about dying and death anxiety. We hope that after having read the chapter, the reader will feel more at home with death and feel more comfortable in approaching dying persons, and thus obtain more access to their life commitment.

APPROACHING ONE'S OWN DEATH

Most of us fear our own eventual decline and demise. In reality, we know nothing at all about how it will feel when our own death is imminent. Might our fear be unjustified?

Several authors have tried to elucidate this question. The following account is based on: (1) professionals who have been present at someone's deathbed; (2) research studies from the deathbed (Kübler-Ross); and (3) people who have themselves been on the verge of dying, but have returned to life (the so-called near-death experiences).

Experiences from the Deathbed

Accounts from relatives and descriptions from nurses, psychologists, priests and others show that the end of life may proceed in very different ways.

> A nurse says: 'I worked in a nursing home where I cared for an old woman. She was up and about, but one day her eyesight failed her. Otherwise she was well. She went to bed and remained there, declaring that now she would never get up again! She had lived long enough. For about eight days she remained in bed in this way whereupon she quietly and peacefully passed away. It was incredibly dignified (...) I have never seen a face so beautiful and peaceful,' says the nurse. 'It was her own choice, and her family was completely supportive of it.'

In this case, the body and the mind seem to be in accord. This woman could say goodbye to life without difficulty.

In other cases, death presents a different face, as in this example provided by another nurse:

> 'I used to work in a hospital cancer ward. One of my patients was a woman of about 30 years of age with cancer of the oesophagus. Her boyfriend was visiting. She knew that she was very ill. Both knew that her condition was terminal.
>
> They went out into the living room for a bit while I was looking in on some other patients. Suddenly her friend came rushing in: 'Come quickly, it's all wrong.'

When we came into the living room, the woman was coughing and hawking up all the blood she had in her body through the mouth. It was a complete explosion. She died in a matter of a few minutes.'

Later on, the nurse elaborates on her account: 'She had become extremely thin, you could almost see her bones through the skin, and her face was completely white. Dying, she sank to the floor. I sat there on the floor, holding her arms and legs. Her friend was standing beside me. I thought: Why did she have to die that way? I thought it was terrible to die that way. And it scared me! It would have been better if she had died slower, in her bed. Not so dramatically. More quietly.'

Death was sudden and came unreasonably early for this woman. Prior to her death, there had been a period during which her body had been attacked by illness.

When the body succumbs to illness early in life, it is often accompanied by considerable distress for the mind, which could have continued to live for many years. Conversely, there are cases where the mind loses its zest for life while the body is still full of vigour. Finally, there are examples of both body and mind being willing to continue, but where life is cut short from the outside, for instance because of a traffic accident.

Kübler-Ross's Theory

Elisabeth Kübler-Ross interviewed about two hundred dying hospitalised patients of all ages to learn what it means to be about to die (Kübler-Ross, 1970). She identified five different reactions in the dying person. She uses the term 'stages', but emphasises that these may come and go interchangeably. *Denial* means not wanting to face reality. Denial is common in connection with shocking news, for example immediately after having been told that one suffers from a fatal disease. Denial may present itself as an unrealistic belief that the diagnosis is wrong, which allows the person to go back to the activities of daily life. Furthermore, *feelings of anger* such as bitterness, rage, envy and jealousy occur. The anger may become intense and may be directed towards the unfairness of life in general and towards any real person who turns up. According to Kübler-Ross, *bargaining* is an attempt to postpone the onset of death by promising a quid pro quo in return for being allowed to experience a specific event or live on for a certain period of time. The term *depression* describes a feeling of grief, dejection and sadness.

The fifth stage is called *acceptance*. Kübler-Ross uses this term to describe a phase in which the person acquiesces and accepts their fate or the natural course of life. The person loses interest in the surroundings and withdraws into themselves. According to many observers, this condition is most commonly seen only during the last few days or hours before the patient dies, and most frequently in elderly people who die in the fullness of life.

Kübler-Ross's theory has found widespread application in training material for health care staff, but there are certain problems with the theory. First of all, the study does not provide basis for a proper stage theory. In this regard, Kübler-Ross is ambiguous. She claims the existence of an actual, fixed sequence of five stages, and she more than implies that the preliminary stages must be lived through in order to reach the final one. Elsewhere, she moderates and modifies. But the theory is often communicated in a rather rigid way and may consequently have the undesired effect that nursing staff become obsessed with identifying prescribed stages instead of opening up, listening and understanding. There is a risk that health care staff develop rigid ideas as to how one *should* die. But in fact, during the terminal stage, the dignified and the humiliating, the ugly and the beautiful often coexist and mingle in a wide variety of ways.

Another problem with the theory is the question of how widely applicable it is. Kübler-Ross developed her theory on the basis of terminal patients studied at a specific location in the USA during the 1960s. These patients were interpreted within a general humanistic and psychoanalytical frame of reference. However, based on this area-specific study, can one generalise the findings to encompass other persons and cultures?

A third problem is the pathologising view inherent in Kübler-Ross's exposition. Concepts such as 'reactive depression', 'anticipatory depression', 'defence mechanisms', 'bargaining like a child', 'projection' and 'the need to work through stages' strike a much too negative and diagnostic note. We are, after all, talking about entirely normal reactions. Negative and diagnostic concepts can easily make professionals blind to positive processes and resources. It would seem more appropriate to speak of grief and despair than of depressions; of hope that comes and goes instead of bargaining like a child; and of struggle instead of defence mechanisms.

Why use disease-oriented terminology at all in order to understand normal life processes? From an existential point of view, death is a perfectly normal phenomenon. Why not express the processes lying at the core of dying like this:

1. If you are going to die, you have to complete your dealings with life. Your ability to do so will depend on how you have experienced your life: Are you satisfied with how things went or can you convince yourself to feel satisfied with them? Have you accomplished your tasks or, if not, can you pass them on to somebody else to take care of? Can you forgive or forget the wounds that were inflicted on you, and have you sincerely apologised for the wounds you came to inflict on others?

2. If you are going to die, you have to let go. To die is to let go of life, to let yourself go as well, to give in, to surrender. The opposite of this is to fight, to resist, to hold on.

3. If you are going to die, you have to relate to bodily pain. To die is often to endure a certain amount of bodily pain and find a way to live with it.

4. If you are going to die, you have to face your anxiety and find a way to live with that, as well.

Interviews with People who have been Close to Dying

Many people have been on the brink of death and then returned to life. Raymond A Moody interviewed more than one thousand people who had had near-death experiences (Moody, 1975, 1989). Related studies have been carried out by Michael B Sabom (1982), Kenneth Ring (1980), Rune Amundsen (1987) and others.

A near-death experience is a person's intense experience of being somewhere else while that person's body is dying or clinically dead. Near-death experiences seem to occur from time to time in connection with traffic and drowning accidents, heart seizures, surgery, war incidents and other sudden, life-threatening experiences. One study indicated that one in 20 adults have supposedly encountered such phenomena (Moody, 1989). But most people usually prefer to keep such experiences to themselves.

Certain elements are recurrent in near-death experiences: (1) The individual's consciousness resides outside of the body. The consciousness can often observe its body from a position a few metres higher up (one may observe one's body on the operating table and subsequently give precise accounts of anatomical and technical details from the operation which can be verified, and which one could seemingly not have experienced on the spot). (2) The individual experiences a feeling of profound peace and freedom from pain (including cases of severe physical injury in car accidents). (3) The individual sees their life flash by and relives a series of important episodes, often in a split second, yet paying intense attention, which implies an acceptance of things past; an acceptance, also, of what has been unpleasant, difficult and perhaps sinister. (4) The individual experiences being present in another world inhabited by people or light beings and experiences being there as infinitely blissful. In this world, the person often meets deceased family members and friends. Being there feels so good that the prospect of having to go back into one's body again (in connection with resuscitation, etc.) may seem distinctly unpleasant.

The following two typical near-death experiences are based on data collected by the Norwegian psychologist Rune Amundsen (1987, pp. 58–59, 45–47). In 1960, a woman from Eastern Norway, then a young girl, had the following experience:

> I was 12 years old and 'drowned' in a swimming pool. As I was about to break through the water's surface to breathe, one of my girlfriends sat down on my

back. At first it was terrible, I felt dead scared. Everything went black and I foundered, was sucked down.

Suddenly I sensed a dark purple light around and above me, and it lifted me up. When I got higher up, the light slowly changed into a rosy colour. I felt I was elevated, that I floated. I saw an infinite white light above me, which was pulling me upwards. It was white, and at the same time I could see each individual colour in it (all the colours in the world). At the same time, I heard the music and songs of 'all times' like a giant symphony, like a cascade. Simultaneously, I could hear each individual song, every hit; I could hear classical music and an organ peal – entire librettos and whole pieces of music – and it wasn't confusing, just divinely beautiful. Peace. Tranquillity. Eternal bliss. The nearer I came to the white light, the louder the music sounded. It was wonderful. I floated, glided and was received. Time didn't exist. I had no experience of my body, just something which was me, and I was in everything.

Everything is like a 'live video' that I'm watching while I write this. I was angry and confused when I was resuscitated under a lot of commotion. Didn't say anything to anyone. Didn't dare to. Furthermore, it was too fantastic for me to be able to share with anyone. Nobody was going to take this away from me by mocking me or laughing at me.

What is interesting here is to see, from a child's perspective, how ordinary temporal and spatial dimensions cease to exist. Note also that categories such as colour and music are experienced as synaesthesia; a simultaneous unity of sight and sound. Such perception is unusual in normal life.

The second example describes the experience of a man from Western Norway. The man is described as down-to-earth and truthful, non-religious, and he has never previously heard about experiences such as these:

After a stressful period, the punishment came in the shape of a thrombus of the heart. I was admitted in the morning and felt worse and worse during the course of the day, evening and night. During the first few days, everything merged, but I think it was during the first night that the major crisis occurred. The pain was intense and this intense pain and a weakening heart function made me lose consciousness. Everything went black.

Then it begins to get light, and I'm rising up from the bed in the horizontal position, floating, weightless. I look down on the white, miserable body that I left lying down there with certain regret. I'm now about 10 metres up and I see a nurse get up from her chair and quickly move towards the bed. She bends over it. I can't see what she's doing, but I see an apparatus and oxygen bottles. She looks at the apparatus (ECG) and at 'that' in the bed. I clearly see her top of hair under her hood. Her skin is white all the way down to the neck. In a way it is not important to me (though I've always enjoyed looking at pretty girls), and I now realise that I'm holding a white rope in my hands. One end reaches down to the bed, the rest is floating in weightless loops. The rope is slowly gliding 'through' my hands, and I'm ascending. I am at the entrance of a tunnel that goes straight up.

It is shaped as if it were made of some sort of cloud. Through the tunnel, what I would call light-music is streaming towards me. There is a new dimension of light and music at one and the same time. It's the most beautiful thing I've ever experienced. Now I'm at the end of the rope and I know that if I let go of it, I'll glide on and up and disappear forever. This makes me think of all the unfinished things 'down there', of my family and all the mess I need to sort out before I can leave. I know that they need me and I start to pull myself downwards. There is no resistance, I 'glide' back into place in my bed, and everything turns dark.

When I woke up again, I looked right into the face of the nurse, who said something like, 'Oh, thank God!' Then the darkness and the pain came back. The experience was clear and distinct. Nothing seemed unnatural. The wonderful 'light-music' and the 'kind warmth' that streamed towards me were fantastic. It was such a fine experience that ever since I have had to admit that I had a glimpse into a dimension that we know nothing about. Obviously, it has given my life a new perspective. There is something at the end of the tunnel.

The experiences described above may be understood in two ways. One possibility is to see them as a result of physical, chemical and biological factors. Near-death experiences may be seen as a hallucination, as a reactivation of a presumed birth experience or as a result of an increased level of carbon dioxide in the blood. Moody mentions a number of these attempts at explanations and finds them all deficient in important ways (Moody, 1989).

The other possibility is to view the near-death experiences as a sign that there is life beyond this life; evidence that there will be something hereafter. From a scientific point of view, the latter is daring and impossible to verify objectively. But a number of medical researchers who are today proponents of this explanation were originally sceptical and incredulous until they inspected the material.

Further clarification of the merits of either conception may be achieved by means of greater research cogency. Extant research does, however, allow one conclusion to be drawn: In many cases, dying is not so terrible as most people think. Sometimes it is downright wonderful. Take for instance death by drowning, which most people associate with a horrifying struggle to breathe, to struggle upwards, and to avoid choking on water. According to the available accounts, the positive aspects of the experience are far more salient than the negative ones, and in certain cases they may acquire a distinctly fascinating quality.

THREE THEORIES OF DEATH ANXIETY

If it is not in itself unpleasant, why do so many people avoid looking death in the eye? Why does death anxiety and the taboo of death pervade our culture and our daily lives? Could it be possible to get on better speaking terms with death? In the following, three theories dealing with this question are reviewed.

Irvin D. Yalom's Theory: Death Anxiety and its Two Defence Mechanisms

Irvin Yalom sets out to reformulate Freud's theory of psychoanalysis, so that death anxiety acquires a central position. 'The fear of death plays a major role in our internal experience,' he says, 'it haunts as does nothing else; it rumbles continuously under the surface, it is a dark, unsettling presence at the rim of consciousness' (Yalom, 1980, p. 27). In order to master death anxiety, each human being must develop specific defence mechanisms. In the treatment of mental problems, much is gained if thoughts about death are allowed to assume a central position.

Like Freud, Yalom works with a basic structure that shapes the part of our mental life that lies beyond our everyday thinking, and like Freud, he thinks along the lines of defence mechanisms. In a thorough and well-documented section, Yalom demonstrates that Freud systematically overlooked death anxiety and instead gave other names to this type of anxiety. According to Yalom, Freud's *Studies in hysteria* (1895/1955) reveal 'an astonishing discrepancy between the case stories and Freud's conclusions and formulations: Death so pervades the clinical histories of these patients that only by a supreme effort of inattention could Freud have omitted it from his discussion of precipitating traumas' (Yalom, 1980, p. 62).

Yalom uses the concept of death anxiety in an approximate way. In point of fact, 'anxiety' designates a condition of terror with no object, while fear is a similar condition directed towards a specific object. Thus death anxiety is a generalised terror of annihilation or non-being, while fear of death is terror of specific death-related events, such as parting with loved ones or physical pain. Yalom finds that death anxiety in its generalised pure form is rarely seen in psychotherapy. Fear of death or defence mechanisms are much more common. Yalom draws an important distinction between two kinds of death anxiety: Either to be aware in principle that we are all going to die (many are able to discuss this and many professionals are especially trained in this type of idle talk about death); or to realise that I specifically am soon going to die (which almost always comes as a horrifying blow).

An important aspect of Yalom's theory is the idea of two defence mechanisms specifically associated with death anxiety (Yalom, 1980, pp. 17ff). The first mechanism is *'specialness'* or *the belief in one's own inviolability*. According to Yalom, everyone believes deep down that mortality is for the others, not for oneself. Most people are convinced that they themselves will not be run over, will not suddenly feel indisposed while out for a swim, will not fall asleep at the wheel of their car. When a person is told that they have a serious illness, the first reaction is often denial or incredulousness. Such a reaction is a way of handling anxiety, but it also originates in a deep conviction of one's own invulnerability. Some people perceive of themselves as exceptions to the laws of nature. 'That won't happen to me,' they think. In this way, they muster up courage to face dangers and risks without being overwhelmed by anxiety. According to Yalom, belief in one's own invulnerability may express itself in a heroic desire to do great things or in workaholism, where the individual is constantly struggling against the clock in order to accomplish more. A self-centred disrespect for others or a consuming need for power and control over others may also be seen.

> As an example of this mechanism, Yalom mentions a 25-year-old male cancer patient who refused to cooperate with chemotherapy treatment, the only thing that could save him. He hated to be dependent on others, hated to be helpless. He had created a life in which he controlled and managed everything himself. Nobody could touch him. At the age of 12, he earned his own keep. At 15, he had left home. After finishing school, he went into the building and contracting industry, and he soon mastered everything himself: carpentry, masonry, plumbing and electrical work. He built several houses, sold them at a high profit, bought a boat, got married and sailed around the world in the boat with his wife.

Yalom's other defence mechanism is called *faith in the great rescuer*. Deep down, many people believe that there is an omnipotent being who will intercede on their behalf; a power or entity that watches over them eternally and loves and protects them. Thus, many people with a fatal disease think that in the last minute, a new miracle drug will be invented. A human being in prison, someone captured by a foreign power or the victim of a shipwreck may think that someone will turn up in the last minute to save them. Some people cower behind their partner, one of their parents or their physician, on whom they bestow magical powers, hoping and believing that this person will be a protective shield against death.

> Another example mentioned by Yalom is that of a 25-year-old man who sought help for an imminent breakdown because his wife was going to leave him. His life was in serious danger: He suffered from panic anxiety, cried for hours on end, couldn't sleep or eat, longed for the suffering to cease whatever the cost, and seriously contemplated taking his own life. He thought about his wife non-stop. He said himself that he did not 'live,' but 'was passing the time' doing crossword puzzles, watching TV, reading newspapers, magazines and engaging in other activities to fill the void and pass the time as painlessly as possible.

According to Yalom, people usually resort to both of the above mechanisms and most people use the mechanisms alternately in order to fend off death anxiety. Thus Yalom sees death anxiety as an immense terror, so powerful and basic that everyone has to protect themselves from it. And the human being uses these defence mechanisms to provide that protection. Many people may become better at facing death, but they will never be able to do so fully and openly. Death is too threatening for that.

Gion Condrau's Theory: Death Anxiety and Longing for Death

Is it necessary to adopt such a negative view of the role of death in human life? Not according to Gion Condrau. In his book, *Man and his death*, he expounds a view that follows in the tradition of Medard Boss and Ludwig Binswanger. Condrau sees a distinctive connection between death anxiety on the one hand and fascination of or longing for death on the other. Anxiety begets fascination. Anxiety and renunciation are also an escape from something that fascinates (Condrau, 1991, pp. 79ff).

Anxiety and longing both form part of the modern human being's relation to death. On the one hand, most people wish to avoid death at all costs by means of state-of-the-art hygiene, inoculations, heart ambulances, organ transplants, life prolongation, etc. On the other hand, our contemporary culture is characterised by forces bent on destroying life; such as unwholesome living, alcohol, nicotine, drugs and an unrelenting work and achievement mentality. Avoiding and courting death go hand in hand. Condrau sees this fascination with or longing for death in many modern lifestyles: in newspapers, on TV and in movies, where we find an immense preoccupation with death. According to Condrau, we should not adopt a negative and condemning attitude towards this. It would be better to legitimise the longing for death and to see it as a positive expression of life.

Condrau then goes on to study death anxiety, its different aspects, its sources and its nature. Anxiety does in fact have many aspects: In one person, worries over what happens after death is continually in focus. In another, it is the suffering that is feared. A third person fears the death process itself. For a fourth person, it is not death itself, but rather the separation from the loved ones that is the uncanny prospect. Some feel terrified by the solitariness of the process or by the fact that death is final. And others fear the outlook of no longer being active and able to make their own decisions.

What is the origin of all these forms of death anxiety? Condrau lists two central sources: The first source is that the individual's life may not have been lived and fulfilled completely. 'Life anxiety and death anxiety may be found in individuals,' he says, 'who have not yet acquired their life potential and therefore have not realised their life. Anxiety is seen wherever life fulfilment has not been realised. This fulfilment may concern to go on living, to satisfy an important need, to complete a given assignment, to allow one's personality to mature or to grow beyond what you are right now' (Condrau, 1991, p. 84). According to Condrau, we feel threatened by the thought that we may have to disappear from this world without really having completed the tasks that were given to us.

Box 5.1   Condrau's Theory of Death Anxiety

Aspects of death anxiety

People are afraid of:

- what happens after death
- suffering when dying
- the death process itself
- the separation from loved ones
- the solitariness of the process
- the fact that death is final
- their inability to make decisions.

Sources of death anxiety

Death anxiety originates from aspects such as:

- I have not lived and fulfilled my life completely; my tasks have not been completed
- modern life in general is risky and does not evolve within a given, value-safe world order.

Nature of death anxiety

Death anxiety:

- is our fundamental anxiety
- is normal, not pathological
- may disguise itself as phobias and other seemingly pathological anxieties
- is about life itself, about being able to *be*, about meeting the world freely and openly.

The second source of death anxiety originates in the insecure plight of the modern human being. In contemporary society, we live exposed and unprotected lives. The individual needs the type of basic security that springs from familiar external circumstances and the conviction that there exists a given world order. Condrau says that ubiquitous anxiety bears witness to a widespread lack of love, 'because anxiety and love are mutually exclusive, if not completely, then to a large degree' (Condrau, 1991, p. 87).

Condrau's view of the nature of anxiety is also interesting. Anxiety is in no way pathological, says Condrau. This remains true even though existential anxiety may prompt the modern human being to consult their psychiatrist, psychologist or psychotherapist or to reach for the drug crouch. Anxiety is ubiquitous, omnipresent. Any effort to eradicate anxiety by psychotherapy is a serious mistake. But psychotherapy may enable a human being to bear and endure the anxiety that life in itself occasions.

It lies in the nature of anxiety that the basic anxiety hides behind other types of anxiety. The fear of flying, mice, elevators or open space may camouflage the individual's basic anxiety. What, then, is the basic anxiety about? It is about life itself. About an inherent desire to gain permission and have the courage merely to *be*. About being free and open, being in one's body, existing in a mood of world-openness.

The human being is always attuned in a specific way. When anxiety determines the attunement, the human being is reduced. The word *anxiety* is related to the Latin verb *ango*, which means I compress, I contract - say, the throat. When a human being experiences anxiety, the throat and chest are contracted, and breathing is impaired. The person no longer respires freely. In the throes of anxiety, a mood reigns that contracts, suppresses and curtails man's relation to the world (Condrau, 1991, pp. 97, 100). Anxiety is an attack on a person's free and open meeting with the world.

Rollo May's Theory: Anxiety, Guilt and Unlived Life

Rollo May defines basic anxiety as the experience of the threat of imminent non-being (May, 1983, p. 109).

According to May, anxiety occurs when there is a *conflict between being and non-being*. Anxiety enters the scene when a new opportunity, a potential, emerges and confronts the individual with a new prospect of unfolding or fulfilling their life. But this opportunity entails the destruction of an established sense of security. Therefore a desire to reject the new opportunity arises. This is where anxiety comes in.

Thus, anxiety is closely connected to freedom. Søren Kierkegaard defines anxiety as 'the dizziness of freedom' and adds that anxiety is the reality of freedom as a potentiality before this freedom has materialised (Kierkegaard, 1844a). In continuation of this, Martin Heidegger says that anxiety offers one of the most basic opportunities to open oneself towards oneself and in this way to find oneself. If a human being does not accept this opportunity, they will fall. This fall means that you escape from yourself, lose yourself in an inauthentic social interaction with the mass. Or you lose yourself by jumping into the busy hustle and bustle of the world and its myriads of things. But what can make human beings so terrified that they choose to escape into the mass or into the frantic rustle of everyday life? Nothing. What causes anxiety is nothing. What makes people feel anxiety is not any specific thing. It is the human, very human being-in-the-world itself. Thus if the individual dares to look anxiety squarely in the eye, anxiety opens up life.

Anxiety is something positive, states Rollo May (1983, p. 112). For anxiety demonstrates the presence of potential, of some new possibility of being that is threatened by non-being. Anxiety emerges when a person is faced with the choice between unfolding or not unfolding a life potentiality. When a human being chooses not to fulfil that potentiality, another feeling sets in: *guilt*. Since human beings will always contain unfulfilled potentialities, guilt, like anxiety, will be something that belongs to everyone's life. Like anxiety, guilt becomes a positive force in life, because it may awaken a human being. Existential psychology thus perceives of guilt and anxiety quite differently from what is usual in the traditional psychoanalytical and psychiatric literature on the subject. In these professions, guilt and anxiety are usually seen as problems and inappropriate formations. In existential psychology, they are basically positive potentialities and guidelines (although of course some of their derivations and distorted forms may cause some initial pain).

The guilt that arises out of an unfulfilled potentiality, of unlived life, is called *existential guilt*. It is a guilt that people feel or harbour in relation to themselves and their own lives. We all carry around a certain amount of existential guilt. Someone whose life is mainly unfulfilled or un-lived will often carry around a huge amount of existential guilt. It may present itself as bitterness, narrowness, dryness, mental sterility and a thorough frustration of the soul. A human being in this condition will often find it difficult to face death and leave life on Earth, for they do not feel fulfilled, but rather feel unused. Examples may be: (1) a human being with a great desire to become an artist or pursue an academic career, but who never did so; (2) a human being who discovered too late in life that they would have liked to have children; (3) a human being who throughout life has had the wrong job, has never found their niche; (4) a human being who has for many years lived under oppressing or unsatisfactory family conditions without being able to correct or break free of them.

Irvin Yalom distinguishes between existential guilt, neurotic guilt and real guilt, as mentioned in Chapter 1. Existential guilt is the person's reaction towards themselves in relation to their more or less unfulfilled life. Neurotic guilt occurs when the individual does something impermissible towards another person in their imagination, or when people transgress social taboos in their imagination. Real guilt emerges when someone does actual damage to another person. It seems reasonable to apply different approaches to these three kinds of guilt. Existential guilt is an important and positive ingredient in the self-reflection of human beings. Neurotic guilt, if it is felt to be a problem, is something that can be worked through, so that irrational fantasies about one's own wickedness, inappropriateness and incompetence can be relinquished. Real guilt should have the consequence that the person seeks to make good for the damage done.

Yalom's, Condrau's and May's theories all offer somewhat different answers to the question of why it is so difficult to face death. In Yalom's world, it is difficult because death itself is and always will be deeply frightening and repugnant to all people. A person can put up their defences, but not change the horror of death. In Condrau's world, the relationship to death is somewhat more positive. Human beings may learn to welcome death, get used to it and allow themselves and others to be fascinated by it and even long for it. According to May, human beings die as they have lived. The higher the degree to which one has lived out one's potential, and the more one has opened up to life's anxiety and guilt, the easier it will be to die.

THE EFFECT OF BEING EXPOSED TO DEATH

Is it desirable or not desirable for a human being to be exposed to an encounter with death? Is it fortunate or unfortunate to witness a disaster? Should we try to avoid such situations? Should we protect our fellow citizens and not least our children and youth against them? Let us take a look at how it affects the further life of a human being that they have had to look death in the eye.

The Aftermath of Near-death Experiences

Several researchers accentuate how having been exposed to a near-death experience profoundly changes the personality and values of the individual in question. A near-death experience is experienced as a fundamentally important life-event. It remains a luminating presence in the mind for the rest of that individual's life.

Raymond Moody, utilizing an anecdotal expository style, mentions specific, frequent personality changes: The individual is no longer afraid of death; gives lower priority to material concerns; places greater emphasis on love and kindness and on being loving and kind; attaches greater importance to gaining knowledge and insight, feels how everything is connected and experiences an opening towards the religious and the spiritual dimensions of life (Moody, 1975, 1989). According to Moody, this increased emphasis on love and knowledge is an important characteristic of the aftermath of a near-death experience.

Other researchers have adopted a more systematic approach. In a detailed analysis of questionnaires from 21 cases, Charles Flynn produces evidence that individuals are regularly influenced in a certain way in specific areas. These recurrent effects are: strongly increased care for others, a markedly reduced death anxiety, a markedly increased belief in life after death and a markedly increased belief that life has an inherent meaning. There is also a much stronger religious orientation. In addition, one often sees a reduced interest in material concerns and less preoccupation with what others might think of you (Flynn, 1984).

In a more comprehensive study, comprising interviews with 102 subjects who had been on the brink of death (52 from serious illness, 26 after a near-fatal accident and 24 from suicide attempts), Kenneth Ring charts a series of corresponding personality changes (Ring, 1980, pp. 139ff). Ring's statistics are not quite transparent, but he seems to find the same effects as Charles Flynn, though perhaps to a lesser extent: Life becomes more cherished, the meaning of life emerges more clearly, the personality is strengthened, and the individuals exhibit a more caring and loving attitude towards other people. He also notes an increased religious feeling, reduced death anxiety and greater faith in life after death.

The research mentioned above exhibits certain methodological weaknesses. There seems to be no doubt that the charted effects mentioned do occur, but it has not yet been established with any certainty how widespread they are.

Effects of Encounters with Death

Irvin Yalom reviews a number of studies that account for positive personality changes after an encounter with death (Yalom, 1980, pp. 33ff). In one of the studies, the researchers interviewed 10 people who had attempted to commit suicide by jumping off the Golden Gate Bridge in San Francisco. Six of these individuals subsequently changed their whole outlook on life. One of them said: 'I was filled with new hope and purpose in being alive (...) I appreciated the miracle of life (...) I experienced a feeling of unity with all things and a oneness with all people.' Yalom's experience with a large number of terminal cancer patients unveils phenomena such as: changed priority of life values, greater ability to choose, to say yes and no, increased ability to live in the here and now, increased pleasure in life's elementary phenomena, deeper communication with one's loved ones, fewer worries about how others see you.

Russell Noyes also carried out a similar, extensive study (Noyes, 1980). Out of 215 interviewees, all of whom had survived a life-threatening incident, 138 stated after-effects that entailed a changed view of life and death. Among the changes were: reduced death anxiety, increased fearlessness and a feeling of invulnerability to danger, a feeling that destiny or God reigns supreme, faith in life after death, greater joy in life and ability to live in the here and now.

Yalom explains these changes by assuming, with Heidegger, that all people have two different ways of living, and that the encounter with death makes many people change from one mode of existence to the other. Normally, most people live in a condition where they forget the big questions. They live engulfed in the myriad of worldly things and forget themselves in the bustling activities of everyday life. They live in a state of *forgetfulness of being*. But once in a while, a human being is thrown out of this routine and thrust into a more unusual state where they pay more attention to life, are more mindful and really feel what it is like to be alive. The essential life events, especially death, for a time move people from a non-aware everyday mode of existence to a profound and attentive mode of existence, a state of *mindfulness of being* (Yalom, 1980, pp. 30ff).

A Danish study has looked into this. One of the most serious Scandinavian disasters in recent years, the *Scandinavian Star* shipwreck in 1990, in which 159 people perished, has been the subject of a follow-up study (Elklit *et al.*, 1995, Chapter 4). The researchers report that two-thirds of the victims of the disaster feel that they have learned something from it. Most of them see this as positive. They mention increased self-confidence and self-recognition, increased ability to live in the here and now and to draw boundaries, increased understanding of other people and improved family relations.

Is There a Life Beyond Death?

Being exposed to death may lead to an increased interest in the religious or spiritual dimensions of life and to an increased belief in a life beyond death. Sooner or later, we all ask the question: Is there a continuation of life after death or not? Medard Boss summarises what people may think about this question (Boss, 1994, pp. 93ff). He offers three logical possibilities: (1) death may be a radical annihilation, there is no more; (2) death may entail a transformation of the former bodily existence into a different mode of existence that cannot be perceived by mortals as long as we are alive on this Earth; and (3) death may imply that the former bodily existence of the person passes on to something that precedes all existence, so that the deceased acquires a relation to being per se that is hidden to the living.

Interestingly, we seem to be living in an age where all of these three perceptions may be found. The following examples derive from the cancer study previously mentioned (Jacobsen *et al.*, 2000); all three are typical ways of relating to these issues:

> A 72-year-old man, a retired artisan, does not speculate about death at all. He has come to terms with turning into nothing after death, 'because all that talk about there being something afterwards, I don't believe that. The day we're done, we're done. When we've been incinerated in the oven then...That's life. And it's the same for everyone. When you slaughter a pig or a horse, it's like that, too. Nothing more will happen to them either, except they might be eaten.'

> A female project manager, 45 years old, is a devout Christian. She says: 'I would very much like to be prepared when I'm going to die. Inside myself, I feel it would be terrible if I died from one day to the next (...) I believe in life after death and that there are higher powers. Something like God sitting in Heaven waiting for you. I think that we are something after death. And therefore I don't want to be cremated, I want to be buried in the good old-fashioned way. I clearly believe that I can go to Heaven if I've behaved well, like being good to other people and caring about one another. And being good to nature and good to animals.'

> A 46-year-old former nurse says: 'I've stopped believing that there is something called premature death. I've stopped regarding death as something cruel and terrible. I don't think energy can be destroyed. I believe that energy can only be transformed. I think that my physical body will disappear. But I do believe that the spark of life – that which has been able to set in motion the process of my entering a body and being born – comes from a unified bundle of energy. That's what I understand by God. That's where everything returns to, I believe.'

When considering what lies beyond life, existential thinkers are divided into two groups. Some (e.g. Yalom and Sartre) see the human being as completely delimited and autonomous: All that exist are people who alone or along with others struggle to shape their lives, to construct their existence. Others (e.g. Frankl and Marcel) see the human being as embedded in a larger structure or totality: there is something outside; a grace, a redeeming, healing or reconciling power (Macquarrie, 1972, pp. 214ff).

Both groups, however, agree that human beings are characterised by willpower and determination. Willpower keeps the human self together, whether or nor human beings form part of a greater whole or not. To focus your activity in a concerted act of willpower is to genuinely become yourself and no longer live absentmindedly in social conformity and the monotony of everyday life. The role of willpower is crucial, a theme to be elaborated on in Chapter 6.

Søren Kierkegaard calls this act of willpower the 'leap of faith'. The human being will have to leap into faith, in spite of reason. The flashing instant in which the leap takes place he calls the moment vis-à-vis God, which to him is simultaneously the moment when the self emerges. To will Christ is to will oneself, he says: 'Now the question is, Wilt thou be offended or wilt thou believe? If thou wilt believe, then thou must pass through the possibility of offence, accept Christianity on any terms. Then 'it is a go' [*es geht*]. So, a fig for the understanding! So you say, 'Whether it now is a help or a torment, I *will* one thing only, I will belong to Christ, I will be a Christian!' (Kierkegaard, 1850, p. 117).

According to Heidegger, it is the moment before death that is essential. Death is not just something negative. To look death resolutely in the eye is to find unity in life. Death sets a limit to my life. Therefore it makes unity possible in my life.

An existential view of that which lies outside can have vastly different contents, as is obvious when you compare Kierkegaard and Heidegger. Many kinds of religiousness or spirituality are possible within the existential matrix.

Recently there has been a discussion in the world community on the balance between religious values on the one hand and freedom of expression in liberal democracies on the other (see for instance www.opendemocracy.net). The question is about the rules of conduct in the public space. To which degree should religious considerations and feelings govern our public space and to which degree individual liberty of expression?

David Wulff has made an overview of the ways of religious thinking of our time and their psychological aspects. 'These are exceptionally interesting times', he writes, '(...) we are witnessing a worldwide resurgence of fundamentalism, on the one hand, and a virtual explosion of interest in the "new spirituality" on the other' (Wulff, 1997, p. v). The existential implication of this development is that even in the modern, secularised countries of the world, religious and spiritual questions are apparently gaining territory, thus requiring of everybody living there that they make their position clear in relation to these matters and develop a consistent world-view, be it secular or religious.

HOW CAN I HELP A DYING PERSON?

A living, healthy person who sets out to help a dying person is facing a most extraordinary task. It makes no difference if the living, healthy person is a nurse, a relative or has some other relation to the dying person. The difficult part is to help someone whose insight in life has moved beyond that of the helper. Can someone who is alive and well even begin to understand what it means to be dying? How can a less experienced person help someone who is more experienced? The basic problem of helping someone who has moved further on along life's path has been discussed by the Swedish gerontologist Lars Tornstam. His theory is that middle-aged professionals have a quite poor understanding of the needs of the elderly, because they cannot transcend their own active and career-oriented life stage and therefore cannot see the real needs of the elderly (Tornstam, 1996).

The way our society is structured, help is needed, and often the helpers are salaried professionals who have helping as part of their job. The help may be given in a hospice, at a hospital or in the home. The helpers may be nurses, doctors, therapists, counsellors, domestic helpers or other staff, but what is said here also to a certain degree applies to family members, friends and voluntary helpers. In the following, I will outline how valuable help can best be given.

Avoid Pursuing your own Agenda with the Dying Person

The helper often has a specific idea as to what is best for the dying person; for instance, that the dying person should be active; should tell their life story; should listen to family members and their attempts to confide; should receive medical treatment; or should be kept quiet with a total relief from pain. Since the dying person is weak and the professional helper strong, it is usually easy for the helper to get their way. This is done with the best of intentions, motivated by a deep conviction of doing the right thing. Often the professional does not realise the effect of their behaviour on the psyche of the dying person, but goes on to treat the next dying person along the same lines, even if the behaviour of the helper is a violation of the needs of the person dying. The helper usually has deeply rooted, personally based assumptions as to what is best for the dying person. These deeply held convictions or beliefs may be so strong that it does not lend itself easily to correction by reality. Here is an example of how professionals may have their own agenda with dying persons:

> An 88-year-old man with double-sided lung cancer had been admitted to an oncological hospital ward. It was clear that he had only a few months left to live. At the physicians' conference, the chief physician suggested radiotherapy, which was agreed. The radiation treatment was hard on the patient, who became weak and felt sick. He begged the nurse intensely to let him off the treatment. All he wanted was to be allowed to die in peace and to be given the opportunity to speak with his loved ones without being overly weakened during their talks. His request was not met.

This example shows a basic presumption that seems to be held by many hospital physicians: initiate treatment at any cost and prolong life for as long as possible. Apparently, some hospital physicians feel that discontinuation of treatment is equivalent to therapeutic failure.

Within terminal and geriatric care, one often sees attempts at keeping the dying person active, engaged and attached to life. It is as if people cannot be allowed to leave this Earth, even if their time has come. Consequently, the dying person cannot really find the peace and tranquillity needed to prepare for the final journey, to attend to their own closure, for they must continually comfort the survivors in their grief. A particularly clear example is the mother who in the last phase refuses visits from her young children. Spouse and staff are disappointed and perhaps outraged, but the mother has said her goodbyes and needs to spend her remaining strength on finishing her own life.

The core of the matter is that the helper must be able to respect the needs of the dying person, even when that person is in denial, is angry or feels sorry for themselves. Not every dying person reaches the point of accepting the final facts. The professional helpers should never postulate rigid norms to the effect that people must die with dignity, or in any other prescribed way. They should accept the dying person's own way.

The Best Help is Simply to be with the Dying Person

Pursuing agendas on behalf of the dying person is an example of a desire to *do* something, of wanting to accomplish something rather than just *being*. Ernesto Spinelli delineates the difference between doing and being, and this distinction is highly valuable and very useful when it comes to helping dying people (Spinelli, 1994, pp. 309ff). Most people in our society, says Spinelli, emphasise what they are good at doing rather than what kind of human beings they are. It is, however, not your doing-qualities that make you valuable to other people; it is your being-qualities. If you only define yourself in relation to what you can do, you reduce yourself to a kind of automaton. The Western human being is used to action. This is particularly true about health care staff when carrying out their work. It is unbelievably difficult just to be with another person, just to be present. The helper's thoughts may travel in all directions; they may be filled with anxious promptings to start tidying up the room; may fall victim to the strange ideas and feelings rummaging about in their head; or may become tense and awkward. Most people find it difficult just to linger, but this is fruitful. If the helper has the courage, lingering together may be of great value to the dying person.

The best way of helping a suffering person is often just to be there, to be present. Presence means to be there physically and to be there mentally as well: to be attentive in a non-demanding way that leaves the other person in peace. To be there for the other also implies to accept and empathise with the other person's world view and priorities. Sometimes the patient attaches crucial importance to a detail that to others seems minuscule, such as to what degree the curtains should be drawn. Here you will have to follow the patient.

To unfold co-being and co-suffering with the patient is the only genuine way of helping the patient further along. If one can grieve with the dying person; be annoyed together with the dying person over what was wasted; be annoyed together over the many times when the dying person said, 'I have to see this and this through before I can start living,' the possibility is there for the dying person to let go. In the words of Arthur Miller (1964), the dying person may finally embrace their life, 'take one's life in one's arms'.

WHAT IS A SERENE RELATIONSHIP TO DEATH?

Heidegger underscores that a realistic incorporation of death as a possibility makes life more genuine. That I am going to die one day is the one fact that I can know with the greatest certainty. Many people would like to postpone death, but death and finality are an essential part of human life. An endless human life would be a monstrosity. It is Heidegger's fundamental view that if death is accepted and anticipated fairly and squarely, it may be a valuable integrating factor in an authentic life (Macquarrie, 1972, pp. 194ff).

According to Medard Boss, people know from an early age that some day, they are going to die. Animals and plants, on the other hand, just end their lives, they cease to be. Because of this knowledge, human beings have to live in a permanent relationship with death. The life of human beings is a being-towards-death.

This being-towards-death (sometimes also called being-unto-death) may take many shapes. Some people flee thoughts about death. The relationship to death may even be characterised by outright fear. But it is also possible to look death in the eye.

Boss notices the fact that children do not normally fear death in the same way as adults. Children do not see themselves as delimited and independent individuals, but sense themselves as parts of a larger whole represented by their parents. Therefore, says Boss, children do not find it so difficult to surrender to death, if that is how things have to be. After puberty, the fear of death often sets in with great force, the more intensively the more the young person sees themselves as an independent, self-contained individual (Boss, 1994, pp. 119ff).

Karl Jaspers describes how we counterbalance our own life account when we approach death. When I face my own death, time has come for me to look back on my life. What stands out in this process as important in my life are the things that I have done or experienced as existential and authentic. What stands out as shaky and ramshackle has been merely external or superficial (Jaspers, 1994, pp. 222ff). Jaspers distinguishes between *existence* and *life itself*. Existence is the external aspects of life that come and go and exist in an objective, material sense. Life itself is that which is experienced and unfolded from within by the free human being. When I face death, I will despair at the loss of my existence, but in the final moment I will recapture life itself. At the moment of death I will relive the things that I have done and experienced as genuinely important. Jaspers seems to believe that this emphasis on what is existentially important compared with what is exterior cannot be made with any finality until the moment of death. At the moment of death, the authentic parts will give life and nourishment to me for the last time; they will give me the possibility of finally embracing my life.

The role played by death in life thus varies from one human being to the next, but it also varies during each individual's course of life. It is as if the individual is engaged in an ever-changing dialogue with death all through life. Death's shape is changeable, says Karl Jaspers (Jaspers, 1994, p. 229). Death's actual shape corresponds to the way I am myself at any one point in my life. I do not just have one lasting picture of death. Rather, my attitude towards death changes as my life changes. Jaspers says: *Death changes with me.*

CHAPTER 6

FREE CHOICE AND THE OBLIGATIONS OF YOUR LIFE REALITY

Modern life is a life of continuous choosing – especially in the affluent parts of the world. Here everybody has to make life's important decisions about education, career, spouse, where to live, as well as a huge number of everyday choices about what food to buy today, what clothes to wear, whom to vote for in the next election, where to go on holiday and what to do in the evenings and weekends.

When clients seek therapy, they are often stuck in situations of choice such as: Should they aim at a divorce or try to endure their marriage? Should they make a major career move? Should they move to the countryside or to another country or state?

In the less privileged parts of the world, life does not present so many choices. People living here basically experience life as things you have to do, comply with or endure; things that are given. For instance, you may have to walk two hours every day to fetch drinking water, you may not be allowed to criticise the authorities, you may not be able to get medical aid, and you may not be able to pick your career or have one at all. Also non-privileged or poor people in the affluent countries of the world often experience their lives as being without choices, just a struggle to survive from one day to the next.

Nevertheless, on closer inspection it becomes clear that you do in fact make choices even if you are less privileged. These choices are not between the free alternatives A and B. What you choose is the attitude with which you will cope with a given fact. You do not, for example, have the choice between various meals; you may get only one modest meal, but you can still choose whether you will say thanks or express your dissatisfaction.

For all of us, therefore, privileged or not, it is relevant to examine what words like choice, freedom, responsibility, necessity and obligation mean to us and to examine how the existential dilemma of free choice versus necessity and obligations presents itself to us human beings in our various social and cultural contexts.

A *choice* or a *decision* occurs when someone faces a situation with more than one possibility, considers the options and ends up by saying yes to one of them, thus not choosing something else.

Choice presupposes freedom. *Freedom* means to be able to do what one wants or believes to be right. Freedom entails autonomy. The opposite is constraint and force. If in a specific situation a person has more than one option, they have freedom of choice or freedom of action.

Choice entails responsibility. When you say yes to one thing and no to something else, this has consequences for others and for yourself. To *be responsible* is to accept the consequences of your own acts. To *live responsibly* means to live in full awareness of the consequences of your own acts. To have or to feel responsibility for something in particular is almost the same as having or feeling an obligation towards it.

When someone is committed to something, the *will* of that person is activated; this in turn leads to *action* when the decision is to be carried out in real life. Sometimes, such a decision can bear resemblance to a *commitment* or a *leap* into the unknown.

An *obligation* is something you have to do, but the term implies that you acknowledge your duty to do it. A *necessity* is something you have to do whether you like it or not.

HOW WE MAKE IMPORTANT LIFE DECISIONS

The most important decisions an individual makes throughout their lifetime are called *existential choices* or *important life decisions*. A number of times during the course of our lifetime, each of us feels that *now* it does in fact matter, *now* it is really important whether I say A or B, yes or no.

This urgency may appear regarding choice of spouse and when the question of divorce arises; when deciding whether or not to bring children into the world; when deliberating choice of career and place of work; questions about travelling and moving; aiming at the unfolding of new skills; choosing retirement or not; accepting the consequences of a certain destiny or treatment that the surroundings have inflicted on you; or other, entirely individual questions.

How do people actually make these important decisions? How do individuals manage to make the right choices? Do we do so through *rational calculations*, by means of listing the pros and cons? Does an *intuitive message* about what is right present itself, either from within or from above? Is the decision made in an entirely different way: by a new, hitherto unknown *part of yourself* emerging and making itself felt? Or do people in fact *slide* into their decisions without much thought so that suddenly, they find themselves in a marriage, with a child or in a certain job?

Examples from Everyday Life

A number of people were given the following task:

> Describe a situation in which you had to make a difficult decision. Describe your considerations and how you arrived at your decision.

The responses show that in important decision-making processes, two polarities often compete, each pulling at the individual. The process ends when one polarity is chosen.

The following example comes from a nurse:

> The Red Cross was looking for nurses for Yugoslavia for an extended period of time. I felt tempted. The area was suffering great hardship, and I've always felt that I should do something to make this a better world. I tried to get my husband and my two children of 16 and 18 to accept my going there on my own. No clear and unambiguous support was forthcoming. I hesitated a lot and speculated whether or not they could do without me and whether my husband would still be there when I came back. I left.
>
> When I came back, I had to recreate my relationship with my family anew, and I'm in the midst of that process right now. One of the children has followed my example and has gone abroad. My work down there came to mean an enormous lot to me. It put everything into perspective. I did the right thing.

The formula for such decision-making seems to be this: *Two incompatible goals are weighed against each other; one of them is chosen, the other is not. Willpower is mobilised in order to reach the desired goal.* Yet another element may be detected in the above example: The two goals are not equal in terms of personal importance. The goal chosen implies some essential life values for this nurse. She would betray her better self, so to speak, if she could not carry out her goal. It is important to note that the opposite choice, to remain at home with her family, might have been the core value for someone else. What is essential here is not a particular type of goal. Deciding what matters depends on the individual. This existential element is clear in the following two examples, both from the hospital sector.

> A department manager was told that one of her employees smelled of alcohol. Several colleagues had commented on it. What was the manager to do? Should she call in the employee for an interview about presumed problems with alcohol or should she pretend she didn't know? The manager says: 'I had to choose

between the easy solution, to let it slide and just be nice, and the unpleasant one, which was to summon the employee to an embarrassing interview. I chose the latter, thinking that was what was expected of me; the situation demanded it, it was my responsibility. It was unpleasant, but afterwards I straightened myself up.'

A young nurse was working together with an older colleague who was also an acquaintance of hers. 'It didn't work out at all,' says the young nurse, 'we just didn't get along. It occurred to me that one of us had to leave. And I was of the opinion, which was difficult to say out loud, that it would be better for the hospital if it was me who stayed. I said it at a staff meeting. She was fired. All my colleagues had been on my side when we chatted in the coffee room. But now they backed down. I felt bad. I made contact with my acquaintance in order to restore our relationship. I succeeded. All in all, the outcome of the story is that I became stronger. I feel that I did the right thing. But my colleagues have also taught me something about human nature.'

In both cases, the choice stands between an easy or pleasant solution, in which the individual just backs down, and a solution that involves doing something which is unpleasant, but also something which seems more appropriate, more reasonable or more responsible.

Other dilemmas may have a different structure. Sometimes the pleasant alternative is also the appropriate thing to do. Sometimes, the solution is not that one of two disputing persons withdraws, but that both stay and work it out together.

Crucial dilemmas often emerge as a choice between two polarities. One is characterised by niceness, social conformity, convention, what people usually do. The other is characterised by life asserting itself and demanding sincerity, honesty, directness, responsibility. Now and then, the actual decision may be based on sheer survival instinct: This is about *my* life. If the individual chooses the non-conventional rather than the conventional road, the outcome of the choice is often resurgent personal strength and a deep conviction of having done the right thing.

The above three examples of decision-making all belong to the type '*conscious weighing of two goals against each other*'. Another type of life decision is '*the breakthrough of a great decision*'. Such a decision matures quietly, but then breaks through suddenly. Here is a clearly expressed example of this type of decision-making:

'The most difficult decision in my life was my divorce,' says a former social worker. The couple had a small boy. 'Our marriage was going downhill fast,' she says. 'I felt bad, and so did our son. And I thought: "This can't be the meaning of life, to – to feel so badly" (...) But I was in a rut in that marriage, and after protracted attempts at communicating with my husband to see if we could improve it, all to no avail, the decision gradually matured: "Right, that's the limit! This is the end of your marriage." And it was just *so* difficult. Because we had Daniel, didn't we? And I remember one morning – we used to have our bedroom in there [*points*] – but I woke up, and I think it was such a beautiful day like today – and the sun was shining into the room, I jumped out of bed, and I got Daniel out of bed and – and then I was standing fully dressed at the foot of the bed where my husband was lying fast asleep, and I woke him up, and then I said: "I'm leaving now!" And that really was a brutal way of doing it, but I had really tried to reach him. He was deeply shaken: "But you can't just leave!" "Yes, I can" (...) It really gave me a sense of security. That I had this apartment, and I did want custody of Daniel. Because it was absolutely plain that I was the one who took care of him. And – it was just so crystal clear to me, that decision; it's as if I can almost smell it! And it wasn't as if I had wanted things to turn out that way. But it was an attempt at making an unbearable situation bearable, wasn't it? (...) First of all, it was all about doing what was best for our son. For who was I to take the boy away from his father? I really had no right to. But I reasoned like this: Since I couldn't stay in the marriage, I had to move on. And I would take responsibility for my own son (...) I wanted out! I felt I was suffocating. I could hardly breathe. And I had been reduced to this imitation of my mother-in-law (...) All I knew was this was it, now – it is almost like that woman Nora in Ibsen's play, where did she go? Like her, I didn't know where to go. All I knew was that I had to get out of that door, and I had to have my child with me. I have never ever stood so firmly on my own two legs as on the day I made that decision. And the sun was shining, and everything was light and friendly (...) I was fed up. I couldn't stay here any more. And the decision had indeed matured for a long time, hadn't it? And then, then I felt: "It is here and it is now!" And I had no second thoughts. "What are you taking, and what are you not taking?" I took my boy by the hand and then we left! We left! And I felt – even though I didn't know where I was going – I felt that we were going out into life! Away from something that was non-life! And I couldn't stand this non-life (...) It took about a year for the decision to take form. About a year. It wasn't something that I just plunged myself into. I had profound considerations. We went out into life; that was exactly what we did. Now I suddenly see that guy Chaplin in my mind's eye – his stride is outward! [*laughs out loud*]. Oh, you just have various pictures in your mind. Of your life. Yes, it was a good day. It really was.'

You get the impression that this decision marks a breakthrough of life itself. A lot of faltering, similar to the previous examples, may have preceded the decision. Nevertheless, this type of decision-making first of all displays spontaneity and power of life.

THEORIES OF DECISION-MAKING

Now, how is it that decisions like those described here can be made at all? What processes are active in the mind? What are the essential elements involved in choosing? In what follows, we briefly review four different conceptions of this process.

Rollo May's Theory

According to Rollo May, the essential decisions are made through a combination of wish and will (May, 1972). For Rollo May, the main problem is the *transition from wish to will*. May defines wish as the imagination playing with the possibility of a certain action or state. He understands will as the individual's ability to organise themselves so that a movement can take place in a certain direction or towards a specific goal.

How do we come from fantasies of something wonderful to the powerful carrying through of one's project? How does the transition from wish to will take place? We can identify three stages.

The first stage is the formation of a wish. To be aware, to sense what is going on in yourself is crucial here. Many people have stopped sensing what goes on in their own body many years ago. Some have blocked out bodily sensations and feelings so effectively that even if they wanted to, they would not be able to sense and feel what they really want. Their upbringing has been too hard on their feelings and sensations. The individual has gone bodily deaf and it will require a long period of repair work to recover the ability to feel and sense. Nonetheless, most people have maintained part of their ability to sense their own wishes and inclinations.

The second stage is the transformation of wish into will. The central element here is consciousness, the fact that we know what we want and would like to do. According to May, this leads to the individual recognising themselves as this-is-me-having-this-wish, as the source of and agent for the wish. Thereby, says May, the will does not become a denial of the wish, but an incorporation of it at a higher level of consciousness (May, 1972, pp. 266–268).

In the third stage, will is transformed to decision and responsibility. May sees decision-making as a coordination of wish and will and their continuation in the form of actual acts and self-realisation. The decision is a commitment: the individual enters into an agreement with themselves concerning a certain endeavour. The previous example of the Red Cross nurse illustrates May's stages.

According to May, wish, will and decision belong together in a chain. The question now is whether May has arrived at the core of the problems with will and decision of our time; or if his contribution should rather be seen as a historically determined cultural criticism. It is interesting how much importance May attaches to wish. He almost seems to be saying that if only you identify your wish as clearly as possible, the rest will follow by itself.

Otto Rank's Theory

We find a different view of will presented by the Austrian, existentially oriented psychoanalyst Otto Rank (Rank, 1968) who, like May, develops his theory of will based on therapeutic experience. According to Rank, the problems connected with making life decisions first of all originate in a lack of willpower. Many people have an insufficiently developed will of their own. In Rank's therapeutic work, the restitution of willpower is a main element. 'It is important', says Rank, 'that the neurotic above all learn to will, discover that he can will without getting guilt feeling on account of willing' (Rank, 1968, p. 9). He goes on to say that the rehabilitation of will solves many problems in one go. For some reason, having and displaying willpower, to have a strong will in itself has been disparaged by many psychologists and psychiatrists. Possessing a will has been fraught with guilt. Yet it is this very power that consciously, positively and creatively shapes the self as well as the surrounding world.

Rank works with building up and strengthening the will of other human beings in several phases. You cannot just say: You must will more. First you must establish a negative will. *Negative will comes before positive will.* According to Rank, this holds true for all child-rearing and all psychological treatment (Rank, 1968; Yalom, 1980, pp. 294ff). The will is developed through three phases: (1) the phase of negative will: The individual is in opposition to the other person's will. What is important here is for the parent or therapist to contain and receive the critical and negative expressions and outbursts. They should not fight them or withdraw, but be present. (2) The phase of positive will: The person wills and truly embraces what they must do. (3) The phase of the creative will: The individual formulates their own wishes and mobilises their willpower in order to carry them through.

Adhering to Rank's principles can be difficult, probably because we live in a culture that is lacking in willpower. Parents, teachers and therapists may themselves suffer from a feeble will unable to express itself with clarity. If the healthy, negative will is to be stimulated in a child, a student or a patient, the most successful outcome will probably be achieved if the parent, teacher or therapist has had their own positive experiences with respectful struggles and enjoyable competition.

John Macquarrie's Point of View

While Rank is interested in individual willpower, John Macquarrie emphasises a different side of the matter (Macquarrie, 1972). The decision is never just the *self-unfoldment* emphasised by Rollo May and Otto Rank. It is also a *renunciation*! To decide in favour of one possibility is always to denounce every other possibility inherent in the situation. Maybe the difficulties modern human beings have making life decisions owe to the fact that they have never learned to renounce. Every single choice in favour of something is also a choice precluding something else.

We shun decisions, says Macquarrie (1972, p. 182). For even though each decision entails that the individual embarks on a new path in life, they are also cut off from other possibilities that have hitherto been open. If you want to say 'yes' to an attractive option, you must simultaneously be able to say 'no' to another option. People's ability to say 'no' tends to be somewhat underdeveloped nowadays. The first three examples from the previous section illustrate this aspect of saying yes to something and no to something else.

Karl Jaspers's Theory

Finally, Karl Jaspers underlines the unique feature that decisions are often made in a certain spontaneous mood (Jaspers, 1994, pp. 181–182). An important choice is often something that seems to just happen. The individual is suffering and has to choose, but the choice to some extent makes itself automatically because greater forces seem to enter the scene. Whether it is nature, life itself or something else at work is impossible to say. But many existential choices are

---

Box 6.1   Theories of Making Life Decisions

Rollo May:

1. Feel the wish

2. Activate your will

3. Make the decision.

Otto Rank: Develop your will in three phases:

1. Realise your negative will

2. Realise your positive will

3. Unfold your creative will.

John Maquarrie:

1. You must first learn to say *no* if you

2. want to be able to say *yes*.

Karl Jaspers:

1. Endure the pain, wait and

2. the decision will break through by itself.

---

made on the basis of the person being in emotional pain and enduring that pain for a period of time. After that, the solution suddenly forms itself, powerfully and convincingly. The art of making important life decisions is in fact to be able to wait, to be able to sustain the ambiguity or the dilemma for long enough for the answer to present itself. A premature and too intellectually belaboured decision will not stand. It is not the will and the intellect that choose. It is life itself that chooses – if I surrender and allow it to. To surrender is a singular, but powerful way of becoming oneself. You could see the last example from the previous section (the woman leaving her husband) as an example of Jaspers' theory.

HOW YOUR DECISIONS AFFECT YOUR WAY OF BEING YOURSELF

We have two possible ways of understanding the relationship between the individual and the decisions they make. Can we say that first the self exists, and then choices and decisions are made in accordance with this, so that the decisions are some sort of logical extension of a self that already exists? Or is it the other way around: The individual chooses first and is then formed by the choice, so that the kind of person that the individual becomes is actually a result of the decisions they make or cannot make? The answer depends, among other things, on your view of the nature of the self. Here we face two different theories that both have their adherents within existential and humanistic psychology.

Theories of a Core Self

According to some theories, human beings have a self that is relatively firm; in other words, you have a substance or core. Carl Rogers is one of the advocates of such a core self. Rogers defines the self as the individual's perception of what characterises them and what characterises their relationships to other people and to the world, including the values that are attached to these experiences (Rogers, 1959, p. 200).

The self and the organism are the two cornerstones of Rogers's theory. There may be congruence or incongruence between the two. The favoured development that he aims to further in both education and therapy is that the two are brought into harmony with one another.

The development of the self is determined by its inherent tendency to self-actualisation. The term self-actualisation, however, rests on the assumption that there is already a self to actualise, if nothing else then the seeds of a self. Whether or not this is the case may be seen as an open question.

The psychoanalyst Heinz Kohut has developed a self-psychology as well (Kohut, 1971, 1977). According to Kohut, each individual has a self that is developed in early childhood; shaped through interaction with the child's most significant adults.

Also, Daniel Stern asserts that each individual has a well-defined self and he holds that this self is developed very early (Stern, 2000).

These theories all propose a concept of the self as something which for the individual is relatively firm and characterises them; something that exists and can be described. They tend to see the individual's choices as a consequence of their self.

Theories of a Relational or Existential Self

Most existential thinkers view the matter somewhat differently. 'It is out of its decisions that the self emerges,' says Macquarrie (1972, pp. 185ff). The decision is a leap into the unknown. What is really chosen, however, is not a thing out there, but oneself.

We do not have a ready-made self at an early stage of development. What is given is a field of possibilities. When I commit myself to possibility A instead of possibility B, I at the same time determine who I am going to become. A human being might say: I want to play music. I want to live with N. I want to move to California. Years later, the individual has been formed by this decision and its consequences. It is in the personally chosen actions that the individual becomes most truly and fully a self (Macquarrie, 1972, p. 188).

Existential thinkers see the self as something that the individual forms through choice and its consequences, something that they bring into existence. The self of a human being is under constant formation. It is created through actions. It is at no time fixed, for it is always becoming.

In addition, some existential thinkers adopt an even more radical position. Ernesto Spinelli seeks to avoid the word self, because in practice you cannot use the word without thinking of a fixed and stable unity, a substance or an essence. He talks instead of the 'self-construct' (Spinelli, 1996). This concept indicates that it is something that you continuously think about yourself, a way of looking at yourself and defining yourself. According to Spinelli, the self-construct does not even exist in isolation, but only in relationships. But if the self exists only in relationships, how, then, would you characterise the self of this person:

> A woman, a former high-school teacher, sees very few people and when she does, she seems to exhibit very different aspects of herself to them. When she's with her weekend boyfriend (an older man), she is girlish and erotic, but also intellectual. With her grown-up child, she is reproachful and dissatisfied, bordering on dismissive. With a former student who visits her regularly, she adopts an affectionate mentor role. With the family members who visit her, she complains

of the state of the world. In relation to doctors and other people in authority, she is quarrelsome and disputatious, bordering on cantankerous. At the same time, she maintains correspondence with several well-known artists, and her letters are characterised by spirit, vivacity and a quaint sense of humour.

One might say that this person shows or exhibits completely different aspects of herself in different relations. Nonetheless, a conversation with her about her life and history seems to indicate, however, that deeper patterns and layers in her self-construct tie together the threads and the relationships.

She sees herself as a woman born with a number of special gifts for literary, intellectual, artistic and erotic excellence. She has only succeeded in realising these gifts to a certain degree. She has a good sensibility for and contact with the themes that preoccupy some of the great writers of our time, but the world has never really appreciated her own gifts and talents. Her immediate family have been unsympathetic or downright hostile and treated her badly. In various workplaces, too, colleagues and superiors have been coarse and uncomprehending.

The story lets us glimpse a basic pattern in this woman's self-construct. She sees herself as endowed with a very special talent meant for a unique role. But the surrounding world is unsympathetic and does not appreciate her talent the way it deserves to be.

According to Spinelli, the individual's self-construct is initially plastic, but through the meeting between person and world it is structured into certain patterns (Spinelli, 1996). The patterns express sedimented opinions or ways of relating that lend to the self-construct a sense of being a more permanent substance. The core of these sediments are beliefs or convictions about the nature of the world and the self. These beliefs hold together the entire self-construct and identity of the individual. The sedimented beliefs, says Spinelli, are the foundational building blocks of our constructed self (Spinelli, 1994, p. 348).

The above-mentioned, basic beliefs or assumptions structure and determine how we interpret a large number of experiences. The term 'basic beliefs' is very similar to the 'basic assumptions' or 'dysfunctional assumptions' of cognitive therapy (see, for instance, Fennell, 1989, pp. 202ff). In existential theory, however, the term 'belief' may also be seen as containing a dimension of personal hope for one's future life. The basic beliefs are often acquired as the individual's solutions to crises and difficult situations throughout their development.

Beliefs such as: 'I'm ugly', 'At least I can solve practical problems', 'I'm very good at all the academic stuff', 'I really know how to deal with the opposite sex', 'I have a bad memory', 'I'm untidy', 'They probably don't want me', 'Everything will probably go wrong', 'I'm no good at chairing meetings', may lie unchallenged at the heart of the self-construct for years and have a great impact on the person's daily life.

Spinelli now points out that these *sedimented beliefs often clash with reality. This opens up an important possibility for personal development.*

Since the dynamic in the sedimented beliefs is incredibly strong, the most common scenario is that reality has to adjust to the belief. This happens because the individual denies or reinterprets whatever aspect of reality that challenges the self-construct. If, for example, the individual has experienced that they are ugly and then receives a sincerely offered compliment, they will easily become dismissive and think that the one paying the compliment is out to gain something. Further, if someone believes that they are extremely good at all things academic and receives a negative evaluation of an assignment, they easily feel hurt and see the criticism as unfair instead of seeing it as a learning experience.

The clash with reality also holds another possibility: the individual may begin to question their many fixed opinions of who they are; what to be or do in future; what they are good at and what they are not good at. The individual may open up inwardly instead of closing down outwardly.

'The opening of any aspect of the self-construct to challenge alters the whole of the self-construct,' says Spinelli (1996, p. 60). And a refurbishing of what kind of person I am and how I see myself paves the way for changes in all the important relations that I am in and live in.

Therefore, entering into a dialogue with someone's self-construct may provoke a protective, restrictive counterreaction because the self-construct is considered so precious by its owner. But it may also become immensely fruitful, because even a small opening can have so many fine consequences.

WHAT DO WE DO WHEN WE CANNOT CHOOSE FREELY?

A very common idea is this: There are many things we human beings are *forced* to do or must do out of necessity. This idea permeates our entire culture. To a certain extent, we all seem to think along these lines. If therapists and teachers rely heavily on this type of thinking, they also tend to reinforce it in the lives of their clients and students.

Is the idea true at all? Do we in fact all *have* to do a lot of things every day? With necessity? Let us try to explore what lies in this idea.

Are there any areas of our lives where we are justified in saying: I was *forced* to do this and that? Very few. We may imagine of torture and other situations where we are beaten up; situations where it is impossible to refuse the bidding of the tormentors. There are related situations where people or their closest kin are threatened with death or injury either in war or warlike situations or by criminal gangs and it seems justified to say: I am forced to do this or to abstain from doing that. Also some of us get exposed to tsunamis, hurricanes and other disasters where we are helpless and can do nothing but run away and try to salvage what can be salvaged. Finally, it seems reasonable to say that if we or our closest family are literally starving and at the verge of not being able to survive, we are forced to try to provide food. In some countries of the world, being forced this way is, alas, a quite common situation. But in the more privileged parts of the world, it is not common any more; it is fortunately unusual.

Also in the many privileged and well-to-do countries and places people often use phrases like 'I am forced to . . .' or 'it is necessary that I . . .' However, such phrases do usually not reflect reality. You are not forced to, you choose to! Admit this, and take responsibility for your choices. We will come back to the advantages of doing so in the last section of this chapter.

IS YOUR PRESENT LIFE DETERMINED BY OUTSIDE FORCES?

Many people are dissatisfied with their lives. From time to time they say to themselves: Now it is time for a change. Or: Next year, things will be different. Birthdays and New Year's Eve are occasions when people are particularly prone to re-examining their lives and making plans for a major change in life. Some people get quite drunk on New Year's Eve because they cannot face the fact that yet another year has passed (and may even have been largely misspent) and cannot clearly see how to make things better.

Is it possible to plan and initiate a major life change? Can a human being freely decide that now things will have to change? Or are we in actual fact determined by forces outside ourselves in the shape of influences from the past or pressures from culture and society?

The existential answer to these questions may appear a little surprising: Whether or not you can in fact initiate a change in your life depends on your own implicit theory about human change.

Does my Childhood Determine my Present Life?

Since Freud, it has been a commonly held belief that the sufferings and qualities that characterise the individual as an adult can be traced back to certain occurrences and conditions in childhood. Throughout the twentieth century, the importance of childhood for adult life has come to be regarded as a self-evident fact; that is, a backdrop for our understanding of ourselves that we take for granted. Today, not only do psychological and psychiatric assessment interviews comprise a clarification of childhood conditions – childhood and upbringing are also a cherished subject of conversations among friends. Magazines and the media in general are rife with articles about the importance of childhood.

Here are some examples of how modern human beings think about their childhood and see their present in relation to their past:

> A female office clerk in her late 30s doesn't experience herself as a free human being: 'I cannot seem to liberate myself from the "nice girl" prototype. I have done a bit of rebellion from time to time (...) but I have to live up to that nice-girl image, the sweet girl – there's that big, nice girl who is so good at helping mummy and looking after the little ones and all that.'

> A middle-aged woman says: 'I'm in the process of liberating myself completely from my father – it has been extremely tough on him; I'm trying to do it as gently as I can, but I'm no longer under his control (...) I feel that to a large extent it has given my life a shove in the direction I want it to have, which is a life in freedom with myself and my surroundings.'

> A man in his late 40s says that his possibilities of living his own life have been 'very, very limited, because I feel that I went straight from being taken care of by my mother (...) and then to being taken care of by my ex-wife. We were divorced when I was 38. It took 5–6 years to get out of that relationship, so it's in fact only during the past 5–6 years that I feel that there's been room for anything else.'

The examples illustrate how some people struggle to free themselves from the influence of childhood, and how that struggle can continue for many years.

The importance of childhood for adult life can be understood in roughly two ways that we shall discuss in the following: a psychoanalytically inspired way and an existential way.

The Psychoanalytically Inspired, Causal View

This view suggests that certain events in childhood *cause* the individual as an adult to be marked by this or that mental state. According to this view, the fact that someone has been dominated by one or both parents in an authoritarian way could lead to the consequence that the adult person becomes dependent and will find it difficult to speak their mind freely. The fact that a child has suffered neglect could lead to a failing ability to love and lacking parenting skills in the person as an adult.

This popular version of Freud's psychoanalytic theory is very commonplace. It is open to discussion, however, what Freud himself would have thought about this causality; indeed, the subject is under current discussion among psychoanalysts.

The psychoanalytically oriented, causal view rests on two components: (1) there exists for a given person one childhood, that is, a fixed core of events and experiences that have actually taken place; and (2) it is possible to draw a direct causal line from these events and experiences (especially traumatic experiences) to specific states in adult life (Boss, 1994, pp. 148ff; Spinelli, 1994, pp. 150ff).

Nowadays, many people experience a strong need to ascertain what their own background was really like. Some want to know how their father or mother actually treated them. Adopted children and children from broken homes wish to clarify obscure points or to know their biological origin. People who feel mistreated would like to know if incest was actually committed or if they were in fact beaten up or subjected to other forms of abuse. They want to know the truth about their past. Why so? The need may be seen as a result of the aforementioned, widely held view that there exists a fixed childhood and that this childhood has a causal effect on adult life.

The idea that childhood experiences determine our adult lives and adult problems originated with Freud's psychoanalysis. For purely methodological reasons, a number of experimental psychologists are quite critical as to the tenability of this theory.

Also, a number of psychoanalysts themselves do not at all adhere to the popular causal version referred to here. Some even adopt a narrative position that comes close to the existential theory that we delineate in the following (Shafer, 1992). But this does not change the fact that the idea of childhood experiences determining our adult lives and adult problems is among the most ingrained psychological ideas in present-day Western societies.

The Existential Conception

This view offers a different understanding of the role of childhood. Each human being has more than one childhood. Stored somewhere in our memory, we all have an almost infinite number of earlier experiences that are in principle accessible to us. Among these experiences we 'choose' to remember a limited number, often of a particular type, hue and basic mood.

Existential thinking sees it as a distortion to superimpose a unidirectional causality on the life of a human being. The mental states and actions of human beings are not caused in the same way as the movements of a billiard ball. The mental states and actions of an individual spring from that individual's *intentions*, from what that person wants in this world. There may well be a *thematic similarity* between abuse I experienced as a child and abuse I experience as an adult, but this does not mean that the former caused the latter. It might as well be that the latter 'caused' the former in the sense that actual abuse that I suffer in my workplace suddenly makes me revive a specific childhood memory from my enormous memory store.

What, then, is the role of childhood viewed from an existential perspective? The role is that the adult uses childhood to define who they are at present. We have all experienced both good and bad moments with our mother and father; we have all been both happy and unhappy as children; we have all experienced both victory and defeat. What we 'choose' to remember as adults from our childhood is that which fits our self-definition or self-construct. If I see myself as successful, optimistic and competent, I tend to 'choose' childhood memories that underpin and motivate this self-construct. If, on the other hand, I see myself as an incompetent, unhappy victim, the memory store from my childhood contains recollections that may support this version (Spinelli, 1994).

This view naturally raises the question of how a specific self-construct is formed or imposed on the individual, and how this self-construct may be changed or developed. Apparently, the theory that fully explains this crucial phenomenon still remains to be developed.

In any event, the childhood of a human being is an interpreted childhood and, as such, is open to re-interpretation. There is no such thing as a non-interpreted childhood; a childhood that was just there. But if childhood is not just there as a fixed entity, what, then, is the reason for many people's search for their roots, for the past, for bygone days, for their origin. How may we understand the desire of so many people to bring out the truth; find out how their parents and siblings really treated them; whether they were beaten; if they were often left to their own devices; if they were properly appreciated and encouraged, etc.? This need may first of all be seen as the individual's way of coming to terms with oneself. To come to terms with oneself entails knowing and accepting the facts of one's life. Secondly, it may be seen as the individual's attempt at getting into contact with split off parts of their personality. The adult often carries around many different moods and feelings that may lie as isolated islands in the mind. The moods and feelings, be they sadness, loneliness, solemnity, warm presence, terror or other feelings from the richness of moods of human life, may be wrapped in a childhood memory that you have only limited access to, but which exerts an attraction. You believe that you are extracting a truth from your past, but really long to reintegrate the split off island in your mind, to get the hidden mood or feeling to belong once again to your conscious mental life.

By contrasting the causal and the existential views, we certainly do not mean to imply that childhood experiences have no influence. Of course they work on and affect and impact on what follows in a multitude of ways. The ways they do this constitute a very interesting field of study. As classical research in developmental psychology, for example the studies by Spitz and Bowlby, has shown, childhood experiences may sometimes have lasting detrimental effects.

However, what we do claim is that for the vast majority of Western adults living today it would be out of place to conceive of themselves as determined by their childhood experiences. For almost all of us, this is a popular belief that we collectively use to keep ourselves in a position where we do not need to take responsibility for our own life, where we do not need to really take our present life challenges seriously. It is a belief that prevents us from making the radical life changes that might be necessary if we really want to become happy.

Do Culture and Society Determine my Present Life?

Another possible lack of freedom lies in the pressure from the others, from the surroundings. Many people seem to shape their lives according to the expectations of the surroundings. They do what 'you' normally do, navigate according to what the rest of the world does.

The problem becomes acute if you wish to live a life different from that of your surroundings. You would like to pursue special interests, live in a more quiet and less stressful manner or perhaps lead a more exiting and adventurous life than most. But is that possible?

> A middle-aged female nursery school teacher says that earlier in her life, she first of all valued looks, money, other people's opinions and to be bright. She let her life be shaped almost entirely by external factors. She often abstained from doing something that she wanted to, thinking: I don't dare, you shouldn't do that sort of thing.
>
> Today, she's trying to live her life the way she wants to. She believes that looks and intelligence have the significance that you yourself attach to them. She now thinks: We're all needed with everything that we contain. And I can contribute to the world with what I contain.

In this case, serious illness entered between the first and second phases in the woman's life. In certain cases, illness can further the process of finding oneself. But even barring serious external events, there are quite a few examples of human development processes in which pressure from the surroundings is replaced by an inner shaping of the personality. Here is one:

> A female clerk in her late 40s describes how at present, she is better able to be herself than before: 'It is age, too (...) you become a bit braver about certain things (...) more secure in yourself (...) I always used to be focused on what people felt and thought about me. I remember one time when I was going to a parents' consultation at my children's school – I removed my nail polish and changed

clothes in order to appear more serious. Today I couldn't care less; people can think about me what they want!'

The question about the extent to which society shapes the individual is a foundational question in sociology and social psychology and has been analysed by a series of the grand old masters of sociology, not least Karl Marx and Emile Durkheim. Also, more recent cultural criticism describes how modern human beings navigate according to the anonymous mass, shape their personality according to the market forces (Fromm, 1947; Riesman, 1974) or narcissistically develop into reflections of the surrounding world (Lasch, 1980).

Existential thinkers discuss this problem, too. Martin Heidegger developed a philosophical theory about our relationship to the anonymous others, which he calls the *'they'*, (*'das Man'*); that is, the others as an impersonal entity, a mass (Heidegger, 1926, pp. 126ff).

Heidegger pays attention to the power that individuals often confer onto others. He does not mean specific others, but others as such. He talks about 'the dictatorship of Others' and thinks about the others as the 'they' prescribing the right way of being and behaving. We take pleasure and enjoy ourselves as *they* take pleasure; we read, see, and judge about literature and art as they see and judge; likewise, we shrink back from the 'great mass' as *they* shrink back; we find 'shocking' what they find shocking, says Heidegger. In the everyday being-with-one-another, we are together with and subjected to the 'they', a non-specific other. 'In this inconspicuousness and unascertainability, the real dictatorship of the "they" is unfolded' (Heidegger, 1926, p. 126).

Is there anything wrong with living a 'they-life', a sceptic might ask, to follow ways and customs, to take heed of established usage? Why should it be wrong to follow the flock or community, to do as the others?

Here, Heidegger points out that the 'they' does not take responsibility. The 'they' only pretends to be able to take a stand on everything, to always be able to say what to do, but the 'they' has no responsibility, for it is not a person. Where there is 'they', says Heidegger, there is nobody. Furthermore, all 'they'-talk is characterised by averageness and restriction: 'They' is always right, but 'they' does not relate to any specific human being or any specific matter (Heidegger, 1926, pp. 127f).

According to Heidegger, all human beings are placed in a life situation in which they follow the anonymous otherness from the very beginning. But we human beings are not *forced* to distractedly hurtle ourselves into hectic 'they'-activity. It is possible to step out of the 'they'-situations in order to discover new possibilities and to pursue them. The individual *can* indeed seize their own self and establish their own course. This is what Heidegger calls authentic living.

The answer to the question of whether culture and society determine the individual is therefore: not necessarily. Only if you let them. In situations big and small, the individual does have a choice. And in decisive moments, human beings really have an opportunity to choose side. This is the existential theory of responsibility which we will now discuss.

CAN YOU TAKE OVER YOUR PRESENT LIFE?

If you want to break the mould of determination from childhood and society on your present life and turn into a self-determining being, the key word is: *responsibility*. What is it to be responsible? When you have to choose between two alternatives, one of them will often be the better one for you. That it is right for you means that it is more in accordance with your basic life values and your goals or mission in life (see Chapter 7). When you are faced with two alternatives, how do you find out which is the right one for you? For instance: Should I buy this flat or car? Should I join that person on a journey to the other side of the globe? Should I marry this person? Should I apply for that job? Or on a lesser scale: Should I take the weekend off to help that person? Should I give money to charity? Should I invite this man or woman for coffee or to the cinema? Should I try to run a marathon? Should I quit smoking? Should I learn mountain climbing? Should I try to get pregnant? If you are considering such questions, how do you find out which answer is the right one for you?

The right answer is to try to get into contact with your deeper life values and ask yourself questions like: If I do this, will I like myself more or less when I look in the mirror tomorrow? And: If I try to picture myself and the way I live five years from now as I look back on what I chose to do today, will I then be proud and happy thinking about myself, or the opposite?

When you try to answer such questions, you assume responsibility. 'Response-ability' literally means ability to respond. To respond means to answer. When you take responsibility, you answer to the requirements that existence imposes on you. You can feel or take responsibility for yourself, for others and for the world as such. We will discuss each of these responsibilities in turn.

Take Responsibility for your own Life

According to Sartre, responsibility is 'the awareness of being the indisputable originator of an event or a thing' (Sartre, 1990, p. 52). It is meaningless to complain, continues Sartre, for there is nothing from the outside that determines what a person feels, lives out or is. If you are in a particular situation, it is because you have chosen that situation (Sartre, 1990, pp. 54ff).You always have the possibility of getting out of the situation or changing it in some way.

There is no situation that cannot be changed. In many cases, it is not possible to change the surrounding world, but in those instances you can change your own reactions and thereby the signals you send into the situation, which in turn transforms the situation itself.

To take responsibility for your own life means to acknowledge your way of life, your choices and omissions. But there is another side to this. In a very fundamental sense, you create the world you live in. To a very significant degree, what you see, perceive and think comes from within, even though it may seem as if it comes from the outside. What you see when you look at a tree or a fellow human being comes mostly from within. Different people see very different things in the 'same' tree and the 'same' human being. Therefore, if I 'see' 'a beautiful tree', 'a poor child' or 'an unpleasant boss', the truth is that most of this comes from myself. What I see is something that I 'do' to the phenomenon I meet. *The individual constitutes or co-constitutes their world and afterwards lets it appear as if it was independent of such constituting.*

Responsibility for my own life then means to become aware of where I, in particular, lay down my own special templates over the world. The hostile phenomena I see and talk about can be disseminated as hostile stereotypes and prejudices to others. The false idyll I see can also be spread to colleagues, friends and neighbours without being at all beneficial to them. The best thing you can do for others is to acknowledge your own shaping, colouring and toning of the world you live in and talk about.

Irvin Yalom describes some frequent mechanisms for *responsibility avoidance*. These are commonplace ways of reacting that the individual employs in order not to take responsibility for their own life (Yalom, 1980, pp. 223ff).

A common form is what Yalom calls *compulsivity*. The individual has the experience of constantly being under the dominion of external forces. People plan their lives so that from morning till night they are running around at everyone's beck and call, trying to fulfil everyone's needs. They do not take the time to sense what they themselves really want and are really living for.

Another form Yalom calls *displacement of responsibility*. This way of reacting is often seen in counselling and therapeutic interviews, but also in the consultation rooms of GPs and nurses and in teaching, etc. The person seeking help does not see the help as help to self-help, which is clearly the most functional and efficient. On the contrary, they delegate the responsibility to the professional they are talking to and expect the professional to come up with and implement a solution, so that the person seeking help does not have to do anything on their own.

Yalom also talks about *denial of responsibility*. An example of this is a person that sees themselves as an innocent victim of certain events even though they have in fact had something to do with these events and have had a chance to influence them. Thus, many people are deeply convinced that it is the spouse, the boss or the colleague that is mean, controlling or egocentric, and that they themselves are good and not to blame. They do not see that mean, controlling or egocentric acts are always played out in a relationship, and that they have their share in that relationship and thereby a chance to change it.

It remains an enigma why we go to such lengths in order to avoid responsibility. What might happen if we acknowledged that we are the authors of our own lives? It would only lead to an acceptance of our own life and being at peace with ourselves.

Distorted concepts of responsibility are ubiquitous: To take responsibility and to live responsibly is not the same thing as being extremely busy doing things for others, it does not mean being self-sacrificing and self-forgetful, not mean frenetically seeing to it that everything is done right, nor ruefully brooding and mulling over all the problems in the world.

To live responsibly is to meet the world freely and openly, to acknowledge yourself as the person you are and to acknowledge why you are here; to breathe freely, look things squarely in the eye, be present. To be responsible is to strike a balance between respect for yourself, respect for others and respect for nature and the world, and to do so with tranquillity and acceptance.

Take Responsibility for the Other Person

Responsibility is not only to acknowledge your own part. It is also to be there actively for others. Let us try to seek out what is means to be there for others.

Gabriel Marcel proposes the concepts of *presence* and *availability*. 'It is an undeniable fact', he writes, 'that there are some people who reveal themselves as 'present' – that is to say at our disposal – when we are in pain or in need to confide in someone, while there are other people who do not give us this feeling.' Marcel goes on to explain how people may be ever so attentive and conscientious and still give me the impression of not quite being present, not really being there for me. Such a person cannot 'make room for me in himself,' he writes, for he is not giving himself, he is refusing himself to me. 'Presence,' he continues, 'is something which reveals itself immediately and unmistakably in a look, a smile, an intonation or a handshake' (Marcel, 1956, pp. 39–40).

Other existential writers have coined similar expressions. Knud E. Løgstrup, who studied with Heidegger, has an apt expression for the desirable attitude towards others. Every time one meets another human being, he says, one is 'holding another person's life in one's hand'. Cradling something in your hand is a metaphor for the comparatively rare situation where you wholly determine the outcome of a crucial situation. So according to this idea, if you meet another person, you ought to be aware that whatever you say and whatever you do may come to have decisive importance for the other person. Therefore you should always think that you hold the other person's life in your hand (Løgstrup, 1956, p. 28).

Words such as these point out a specific attitude and quality that someone may exhibit towards someone else. Inspired by Martin Heidegger, Rollo May has tried to narrow down this state using the word *care* (May, 1972, pp. 289–293). According to May, care, as opposed to indifference and apathy, is the circumstance in which someone or something means something to you. Care is the source of human tenderness. Care is also a basic feature of human life. We are born in care and to care. A human being cannot live without care.

Care is scarce these days, says May. Emotional coldness, apathy and lack of commitment have become rampant. But you need to distinguish between genuine care on the one hand and false care or sentimentality on the other. Sentimentality is to think about your own feeling rather than experiencing what the feeling is directed towards. The sentimental individual thinks: I *have* this feeling and dwell in it; perhaps I want to share it with others, talk about my feeling. The caring and responsible person *directs* their feelings towards something and is present and close to any person or thing which the feeling is directed at.

This distinction between genuine and false care is important. Some professionals seem to believe that if they cannot make their patients or students talk about their problems, there is something wrong that has to be mended. Such an attitude is not genuine care. Genuine care is to let the other person be and respect the other person's wish for something different than what you offer. Care is to want the best for the other person, not as an extension of yourself, but showing respect for the other person's integrity and autonomy. To care and take responsibility for someone else is a dual act: The caring person goes in for the other person, throws their lot in for the other person, does something for the other. At the same time, the caring person lets the other be, waits, is attentive, pauses, follows with interest, lets the other unfold, observes. Genuine care is doing and being rolled into one.

Take Responsibility for the World

It is often discussed how much or how little the individual should get involved in the big issues. Is it reasonable or unnecessary to worry about the depletion of natural resources and the exploitation of the eco-balance? Or about the wars and the poverty around the world?

To take responsibility for the world is to be affected by the condition of the rest of the world. Knud E Løgstrup has argued that human beings live in a fundamental *interdependence*, a mutual dependence of the rest of the world and that it is therefore a permanent life task to relate to the world (Løgstrup, 1956, p. 14).

Many people find it difficult to commit themselves to the world at large. It is as if the global problems seem too overwhelming. Therefore, many people turn their backs on the overpowering world to concentrate instead on the microcosm of private life and private feelings among a few people. To connect the little private world with the large public world seems quite difficult for most people, and there may at present be a lack of public models for and examples of how to do so in a constructive way (Jacobsen, 1989). Interestingly enough, one of the paths leading towards that kind of world commitment (or world citizenship) may well be through a mixture of existential group work and adult education (Jacobsen, 1997).

Yet, we live in an age where it has become normal to believe that it does not matter whether we commit ourselves to the big issues. Many people would in fact like to commit themselves more, but do not know how to or cannot find the time for it. They imagine that such a commitment might drain their personal energy rather than replenishing it, in spite of experience showing that the opposite is most often the case: In general, people tend to feel stimulated and get a certain jolt of energy when participating in political or citizen-based grass-root work.

To some extent, the passive people suffer from a specific form of erroneous thinking. Paulo Freire calls this type of thinking mechanistic objectivism. People of this persuasion, he says, believe that reality transforms itself without human acts. These people see human beings as mere pawns subjected to the changes of the world. They do not see that human beings can transform the world and be decisive in historic processes of change.

You cannot, says Freire, observe the world in itself independently of the men and women that constitute it, live in it, create it: Humans and the objective world are two polarities in a dialectic relationship. 'The two come together as unfinished products in a permanent relationship in which human beings transform the world and undergo the effects of their transformation' (Freire, 1976, p. 145).

But how can we receive and contain the happenings of the global world? Jon Kabat-Zinn from the stress clinic at the University of Massachusetts calls this challenge to meet the 'world stress'. 'To have a positive effect on the problems of the larger environment', he writes, 'we will need continually to tune and retune to our own center, cultivating awareness and harmony in our individual lives' (Kabat-Zinn, pp. 417 ff). He advocates trying to pay attention to the amount and quality of information we take in through newspapers and television and becoming aware of how it affects us. He also recommends that we try to identify specific issues that we care about. 'Just doing something', he writes, 'even if it is a very "little" something, can often help you to feel as if you can have an effect, that your actions count, and that you are connected to the greater world in meaningful ways (...). Since you are a part of the larger whole, it can be inwardly healing to take some responsibility for outward healing in the world'.

CHAPTER 7

TO FIND THE MEANING OF LIFE IN A CHAOTIC WORLD

LIFE GOALS, LIFE MEANINGS AND LIFE VALUES

The life of the modern individual has no pre-defined meaning. From time to time, modern human beings ask themselves why they live at all. They reflect on their life values and on how to make their priorities.

Fifty to a hundred years ago there was a given meaning. The meaning of events was passed on by tradition, and each person was told what everything was all about. The priest, family members and neighbours could explain what had really happened when crisis struck, and the unfortunate victim was told how they could cope. The rules of life and its meaning were laid down in advance in our cultural patterns.

For someone born in our times, however, the meaning of life is a vacuum that we have to fill out for ourselves. The threat of depression and even suicide lurks in the lives of those who are not able to fill this void. Our culture offers many possible ways of bestowing meaning on existence, but each individual has to actively choose a way to construct the meaning of their own particular life. Only when people are able to accomplish this task with conviction and commitment do their lives seem to gain coherence.

So the modern human being lives with a difficult dilemma: how to find or construct a meaning where none is given beforehand. It is a dilemma that involves searching, choosing and committing oneself to goals and meanings on the one hand and the prospect of falling back on despair, meaninglessness and a state of everything being equally right or wrong on the other.

How, then, do people go about the task of finding or creating the meaning of their lives? Why is it easy for some, while others see their lives fall apart? Life is meaningful for people when they can see a pattern or purpose in the events of their lives. Conversely, it is meaningless when things seem to crumble and you cannot see the sense behind what you do or behind the events that fill up your life.

The term *life meaning* refers to the content with which people fill their lives. Life meaning imbues life with form and direction. A related concept is *life goal*. It refers to the objectives that people work towards and try to achieve. A person may have the life goal of becoming an actor. In that event, the experience of being part of the pulsating life of a theatre and sharing in its artistic endeavours will provide life meaning for that person.

Life meaning and life goals are selected by each individual in accordance with more basic *life values*. Life values refer to the particular visions of the good life that form the basis of the life of an individual. Love, for example, can be a life value. A person inspired by this life value can set out to pursue the more specific life goals of building a partnership and having a family.

WHAT LIFE GOALS AND MEANINGS DO PEOPLE HAVE?

When people are asked about their goals in life, they come up with very different answers. Examples of some typical responses taken from a research project are shown in Box 7.1.

These answers have some striking aspects. The goals are quite different. They range from things the person hopes to obtain to characteristics the person hopes to develop. Also, the tone of the responses differs. The phrases reflect the individual language of each person. The number of stated goals also varies – expressing perhaps the age of the respondents and their appetite for life. Finally, it is as though these brief responses say something significant about each person; as if, in stating our life goals, we express some core aspect of ourselves.

Life goals questionnaire

A number of psychologists have attempted to develop methods for charting the variety of life goals. A questionnaire enables us to make comparisons that can be utilised for research purposes or as a basis for personal reflection. There is a risk, of course, that a questionnaire will not really capture the essence of what life is for a given person. Handled sensibly, however, such a questionnaire can assist you in the process of self-understanding and that of understanding other people.

A questionnaire of this kind, developed by the author, is shown in Box 7.2.

As an example, we may look at the answers provided by a 56-year-old lawyer, a married man with grown-up children and a job that involves him with issues of social policy. It emerges from his completed questionnaire that goals related

---

Box 7.1   Examples of Life Goals

How would you describe your goals in life? Artist, man, 67:

1. that my work will go well,

2. that I'll find a partner with a bit of spark – someone I can travel with and share all kinds of experiences with,

3. a Spider Alpha Romeo – I love toys and I adore fast cars.

Shopkeeper, man, 46:

1. that my family will be safe and sound and stay healthy and well,

2. that we can hang on to the security we have at the moment, without any accidents happening to us.

Secondary school teacher, woman, 46:

1. that I can become a bit more out-going in my relationships with other people,

2. that I would be able to feel more free,

3. that I would do more things because I really want to do them, rather than because I feel duty-bound.

Nurse, man, 25:

1. that the baby we are expecting will be healthy and well,

2. a house in the country near the woods and water,

3. that we won't be too pushed for money,

4. to travel overseas and meet other people,

5. that my family and friends will have a long life and not become sick,

6. that I myself will have a good life, free of illness, and that I will have a long life and stay vivacious to the end.

---

to work, material conditions of life and personal economy are placed relatively far down on his list of priorities. Family life, on the other hand, ranks high for this person, as well as a desire to mean something to other people and to be able to make some contribution to society.

Box 7.2   Questionnaire of Life Goals

If I can't achieve everything in this life, the *most important* must be:

Attach a number to each item according to its importance (1 for the most important, etc.)

a.   to achieve something at work .... ☐

b.   to have good material conditions and a sound economy ...... ☐

c.   to have a good family life .... ☐

d.   to have an eventful life with many different kinds of experience (music, nature, travel, art, friendships, etc.) .... ☐

e.   to make a contribution to society, so that the world in some small way will become a better place to be .... ☐

f.   to live in accordance with some greater religious or spiritual idea .... ☐

g.   to be free from serious illness and misfortune .... ☐

h.   to develop harmoniously in accordance with my inner self ...... ☐

i.   to develop intellectually and to acquire new knowledge .... ☐

j.   to mean something to other people and to help others .... ☐

k.   to accept my lot in life with dignity .... ☐

Different occupational groups tend to complete this questionnaire in different ways. Nurses, for instance, tend to value the goals of developing themselves harmoniously, having a good family life and to meaning something to other people. Other occupational groups display a different kind of profile, although always with individual variations.

Age is also significant. Very young adults such as young students often attach importance to an eventful life. A slightly older age group tends to attach high priority to a good family life. Some older adults prioritise their intellectual development or the religious dimension of their lives.

The questionnaire can also shed some light on relational problems. One woman participant in a seminar had asked her husband to complete the questionnaire as well. To her astonishment, this exercise revealed to her why they so frequently disagreed: Their life values were miles apart.

The life goals people harbour and their more fundamental life values can be gleaned from the way in which they complete a questionnaire of this kind. But is it possible to create a theoretical system that presents the life values of human beings in a systematic overview? Gordon W Allport, the well-known American psychologist, has made an attempt in preparing a catalogue of our basic life values (Allport, 1961, pp. 294–300).

Allport's Theory

Allport differentiates between six types of people, classified according to what the person lives for. The theory refers to pure types.

1. *The theoretical person* lives to discover or uncover truth. The most important thing in life for the theoretician is to seek knowledge and insight, or to somehow show others the path to truth. Research and teaching are among the occupations in which this life goal can be awarded priority. Other occupational groups can also find their leisure time pursuits in this area.

2. *The economic person* is oriented towards the utility of things. What counts for this person is the use to which something can be put and the monetary value that is placed on it. To create a profit, to see one's business or bank account grow is what matters. Occupations in the sphere of business offer opportunities to develop this orientation in life.

3. *The aesthetic person* is oriented towards the forms and harmonies of things. Beauty is what matters to this person. Life is seen as events and impressions that can be enjoyed for their own sake. Living for the sake of beauty can be realised in such occupations as artist, architect, craftsman or designer. The aesthetic dimension can also play an important part in the leisure time activities and in the homes of persons belonging to other occupational groups.

4. *The social person* cultivates love for and affinity with other people as the life value that has highest priority. This person wants to mean something to other people and to help them. Occupations as care persons and many other occupations in the health and social sectors offer opportunities to realise this life value. But many other people, including housewives, unemployed persons, voluntary workers and people who are active in grass-roots organisations also have ample opportunity to develop this social orientation.

5. *The political person* is interested in power. What is important for this person is the ability to place themselves in a position of power and to exercise influence over other people. An occupation as politician offers the opportunity to pursue this life value in a relatively pure form. But many other occupations as well as voluntary work in organisations offer ample scope for cultivating an interest in the pursuit of power.

6. *The religious person* seeks unity with something that lies beyond the everyday world. This quest may take the form of adhering to the practices of a particular religion or of aspiring to find some other form of spirituality that is less clearly defined. Occupations in the sphere of the church, such as that of priest, can offer an opportunity to realise this dimension in life. A very wide spectrum of leisure time activities, ranging from voluntary work on a parish council to

the practice of yoga, can also provide a framework within which a search for spirituality can take place.

Some people seem to exemplify one of the pure types identified by Allport, but many people represent a mixture of types. Think for example of a university teacher who starts a business firm, an architect who specialises in church design or a nurse who becomes involved in trade union activities.

Are All Life Goals Equally Important? Erich Fromm's Theory

As we saw above, Allport distinguishes six types, placing them on an equal footing. He makes no judgement as to whether one type is more necessary or more valuable than another. Perhaps, from his point of view, all six types represent necessary contributions to the maintenance and development of a harmonious society. Or perhaps he sees these six ways of life as belonging to a natural order that should be respected, in much the same way as we respect the existence of animal or plant species. But are these life values equally worthwhile? Is the task of making money just as valuable as that of seeking spiritual fulfilment? Is the search for beauty just as precious as the search for love? Or, to return to the questionnaire, is the task of developing harmoniously in accordance with one's inner self just as important as that of achievement at work? We may discriminate between three viewpoints on this issue.

The *viewpoint of neutrality* maintains a principle of equal value. A person who espouses one life value cannot be the judge of another person who happens to have chosen differently. No one may claim the superiority of one kind of life goal or life value, pronouncing that one way of life is better or more worthwhile than another.

The *viewpoint of commitment* can be found in the works of Jean-Paul Sartre (Sartre, 1990, pp. 52ff), but also in Søren Kierkegaard's conception of choice as a leap. According to this view, what matters is not the particular choice. A person may live for their work or strive to obtain inner harmony. What counts is the manner in which a person commits themselves to a chosen way of life. People who devote themselves wholeheartedly to their work do so in an authentic way. Those who go about their work in a half-hearted manner will tend to feel alienated from their work to some extent.

The *viewpoint of necessity* maintains that certain goals should be preferred in so far as they are needed by the world around us. People should not, therefore, choose with complete freedom, merely according to their inclinations. Not all possibilities are in fact equally worthwhile. In our day and age, conditions in the world around us may be such that some ways of life should be given preference, while others should be seen as less fortunate choices.

This is the approach taken in the book *To have or to be?* by Erich Fromm (1976). Fromm presents two fundamentally opposed modes of existence for our consideration, one oriented towards having and owning, the other towards being and living. He points out that a number of ordinary, everyday activities (learning, remembering, conversing, etc.) change character according to whether they are undertaken in one or the other of these modes. When the mode of having is dominant, love for others will tend to be expressed in the form of setting limits, seeking to control others, to own them and to have rights over them. Loving acts take a different form when undertaken in the mode of being. They will then tend to focus on the enjoyment of being together, of giving to each other and inspiring each other (Fromm, 1976, pp. 28ff).

According to Fromm, the mode of having thrives in a society that is organised around the tasks of acquiring, owning and yielding profits. The feeling of ownership embraces one's property, but also one's name, one's body, social status, knowledge and family. This mode of existence refers to things that are fixed and describable.

The mode of being on the other hand refers to lived experience. To be, according to Fromm, involves opening oneself to the world and relinquishing any tendency to egoism.

Both of these modes of existence are possible choices, given human nature. Fromm holds the view that there are excellent reasons for seeking to limit the influence of the having mode of existence, while seeking to promote the being mode. Unless people's habits can be turned away from the mode of having towards that of being, an environmental disaster threatens all of us on a global scale. 'For the first time in history, the *physical survival of the human race depends on a radical change of the human heart*,' writes Fromm (1976, p. 19, original emphasis). To this, however, he adds the observation that the human heart can only be changed when economic and social conditions are changed at the same time.

Other authors think along similar lines, seeking to clarify the relationship between global awareness on the one hand and a psychological theory of human development on the other. According to the French philosopher and sociologist Edgar Morin, it is necessary to exert an influence on the thought patterns of the individual if we are to ward off a global cataclysm (Morin, 1973, pp. 363ff; Morin & Kern, 1993). But at the same time as a reorientation takes place on the individual level, the structures of society must also be changed in a way making societies more genuinely human – more organized in accordance with the being mode of existence as identified by Fromm.

In his contribution to the theory of education, the Brazilian existential thinker Paulo Freire also argues that the mentality of the individual and the structure of society must undergo a simultaneous and reciprocal process of change

(Freire, 1976, pp. 3ff, 143ff). There is a need to establish dialogue, mutual respect and an open, exploratory form of discussion on the micro-level of the group. On the macro-level of societies and nations, there is a corresponding need to reduce the incidence of violence and exploitation and to promote mutual respect and agreement.

Let us return to the question posed at the outset. Is one life value and life meaning just as good as the next? According to Allport, the answer would seem to be yes, it is. We should remain neutral in the face of value judgements. We should respect the natural differences in human inclinations. According to Fromm, Freire and Morin, however, the answer seems to be no. Certainly, everyone has to take into account their own abilities, inclinations and options. But everyone should also take into account the global conditions of survival and the need for a more humane society.

DO GOALS AND MEANINGS CHANGE DURING THE COURSE OF LIFE?

Theories of Stages

Do different life meanings and life values belong to particular stages in the course of life? Or do people pursue ways of life that have nothing to do with their chronological age?

It is often said that young people have their own patterns of behaviour (getting blind drunk, for example, behaving foolishly or outlandishly). Other patterns belong to old age (a protracted conversational style for instance, or the tendency to accept misfortune with quiet resignation). The idea of fixed patterns of behaviour as being suited to a particular age-group are no longer taken for granted these days. The answers to the questionnaire in Box 7.2 demonstrated that life goals do tend to change with age, but not according to any standardised formula. For instance, some people subscribe to the view that a good family life is a goal that is over and done with when the kids leave home. Yet others retain the goal of having a good family life for the rest of their lives. For some people, the goal of intellectual development is one that belongs to their early 20s, while others adopt it as a priority in their 50s.

Several psychologists have developed theories regarding changes in goals and values that occur during the course of life. Such theories of change have been put forward by Charlotte Bühler (Bühler, 1959; Bühler & Massarik, 1968) and C.G. Jung (see Jacobi, 1983, pp. 21ff), among others, as also explicated in Chapter 3. Both Bühler and Jung developed the theory (first advanced by Jung) that a tendency to evaluate one's life is characteristic of the middle years of the life cycle. This evaluation may unfold during a crisis and will then decide the course of the life that follows. According to Jung, the development of the individual – the process of individuation – comprises two main phases, corresponding to the first and second half of the life cycle, often bridged by a so-called mid-life crisis. The way of life pursued in the second phase can be diametrically opposed to the first.

Charlotte Bühler subdivides the life cycle into five phases, each distinguished by the person's concern with life goals. Among these is the phase from approximately 15–25 years of age, during which the person seeks out and makes preliminary decisions regarding their life goal. The next phase comprises the years from approximately 25 until 45 or 50, during which the person's decisions with regard to their life goals become increasingly specific and definitive. This is followed by an evaluation of the life that has been led thus far, possibly resulting in a change of direction being planned for the remaining years, ensuring that important goals can indeed be reached before it is too late.

Søren Kierkegaard also presents an account of the stages of our lives, most clearly expressed in *Stages on life's way* (Kierkegaard, 1845). In this work, he identifies three ways of relating to the world and describes them with a sympathetic insight into the characteristics of each, an insight that remains quite extraordinary. These stages are called the aesthetic, the ethical and the religious, respectively. As he sees it, these stages may succeed each other in the order mentioned in the life of the individual. Each successive stage represents a more enlightened form of life. Kierkegaard's stages are regarded as a major contribution to world literature and philosophy. They also represent a psychological theory that, strangely enough, never seems to have been subjected to empirical study.

Frankl's Theory

The theories of Bühler and Jung do not tell us at what stage in the course of the life cycle the particular life goals tend to be pursued. The Austrian existential psychiatrist, Viktor Frankl, has made an important contribution here.

In Frankl's view, the primary driving force of a human being is the individual's search for meaning. He describes this search as the will to meaning, and he notes that people are prepared to live and die for the sake of ideals and values (Frankl, 1959). Frankl employs a number of case studies to demonstrate the fact that this will to meaning can sometimes exert an influence that is very much greater than the instinctual drives described by Freud. As Frankl sees it, human consciousness is never wholly formed by the influences from the person's environment. In his own words: 'A human being is not one thing among other things; *things* determine each other, but *man* is ultimately self-determining. What he becomes – within the limits of endowment and environment – he has made out of himself' (Frankl, 1959, p. 135).

People fulfil their personal existence by realising values. To live is to pursue a meaning in life, to struggle towards an important goal, to realise a value. Let us look at what kind of values people try to manifest, thereby giving content, shape and form to their lives. Frankl pinpoints three kinds of values.

The *creative values* are realised in activities such as constructing and giving and are pursued in the spheres of work and family life. These values have an expansive character, tending to enlarge as well as establish the person's world.

The *experiential values* are realised in the ability to open oneself to the world and to respond to nature, art and love. To realise such values is to lead a life that is rich in experience. These values have a receptive character, that of letting the world in.

The *attitudinal values* are realised in the ability to prepare oneself for the limitations of circumstance, the reality of suffering or perhaps the renunciation needed to cope with a harsh fate. These values come into play in the face of illness or approaching death. We also call on them when we have to abandon other goals we failed to achieve. It then becomes a task in itself to be able to accept our fate and to find a meaning in that circumstance. According to Frankl, a human life retains its meaningful character to the last second of existence, right until the final breath has been drawn. We give priority to the more active values as long as we can. Values that are linked to suffering only enter the picture when forced by necessity: 'The destiny a person suffers therefore has a twofold meaning, to be shaped where possible, and to be endured where necessary' (Frankl, 1966, pp. 111–112).

Frankl's account of these three kinds of life values sums up what people live for in our age. Each type of value is different in character and seems to correspond to a particular manner in which the human psyche functions. As Frankl understands it, each type tends to come into play in a given chronological order. The usual pattern is one whereby people try to realise the creative, expansive values while they are young, striving to mould their existence through their work and by building a family. Later in life, people tend to be more receptive to the values of experience as enjoyed in nature, art and the experience of loving. Towards the end of life, when fate may be less kind, they are presented with the task of finding a meaning in their suffering.

This particular order of events may of course be relatively common. But it does not seem quite justified to present it as a development that necessarily occurs in a given chronological sequence. A number of young people these days, for instance, do not succeed in finding a place in the educational system or in the labour market. In that event, they will tend to orient their lives towards the values of experience instead. People who initially embark on their adult lives in this way may very well, at a later stage in their lives, pursue creative, expansive activities and values. There are also a considerable number of children and young people who have to find ways of dealing with suffering at an early point in their lives, perhaps due to serious illness. Thus Frankl's attitudinal values may in this way come into play for these young people prior to any search for other values.

Given these reservations, Frankl's theory can be accepted in all its simplicity. His concepts have the advantage that they encompass many of the kinds of goals that people actually do pursue in their lives. This theory also indicates that when people strive to realise one of these values in their own lives, the process seems to involve a corresponding development of their psyche, a new way of being in the world.

Changes in Goals and Meanings Following Significant Life Events

Life goals and life meanings do tend to change during the normal course of the life cycle. But does the meaning of a person's life also change if it is suddenly affected by outer circumstance? What happens to a person's life goals, if accident, a serious illness or the death of a close relative suddenly looms on the horizon? We analysed the phenomenon of crisis in Chapter 4, but other significant life events also entail special consequences in relation to the meaning of life.

Sudden shock due to some outer circumstance may affect a person in one of two ways. The person's way of life and pattern of activity can be brought to a standstill as though frozen in time. Alternatively, an intensification of personal development can occur. It is difficult to say how frequently the frozen reaction occurs, compared with that of intense development. But the latter reaction is by no means unusual. It involves certain processes that are of particular psychological interest. Consider for example the following answers to a question about the meaning of their lives given by one person who is in the best of health and two others who are seriously ill (Box 7.3).

The response from the person enjoying good health differs from the answers from those who are seriously ill. This is not unusual. The style and tone, as well as the content and level of detail, do tend to differ between persons who are well and those who are sick. The life meanings of seriously ill persons tend to focus on their relationships to the people to whom they feel closest, as well as on their relationship to themselves and their immediate surroundings. There seems to be a particular tone in their responses that is more introverted and more reflective. The desire to pass on experience and values becomes crucial. This can be seen as one of the ways of finding a meaning in the experience of being ill.

Box 7.3   Examples of Life Meaning

How would you describe the meaning of your life?

Shopkeeper, 55, woman in good health:

> We are put into this world in order to accomplish something or other which we need not feel ashamed of at the end of our lives. We all have to achieve something. Achieving something is what it's all about – doing a decent bit of work.

Nurse, 41, seriously ill woman:

> First of all, the meaning of life for me as a person here on earth is to be here and to be able to accept and to give love. And then, for me in particular, I think it's to be able to pass on some of my experience.

Project manager, 44 years old, seriously ill woman:

> To play some part in making the world a better place – to form the lives of children and young people in a way that makes it possible for them to live in harmony with nature and the planet we are living on. I feel a responsibility for that, for schooling, the society around me and for the environment. I would like to be able to pass on some of my experience, also to people of my own age. A lot of people my age have allowed their lives to pass by, I think, without trying to influence anything. And then I would like to give my children a really good start in life, so that they will have good lives later on – lives they find satisfying and in which they accept responsibility for the things they do.

Are the Stages of Life Laid out in Advance?

An important question arises when considering the stages of the life cycle of the adult as described by Bühler, Jung, Frankl and Kierkegaard. If the life cycle leads to a more advanced stage towards the end of life, would it then be a good idea to make a conscious effort to reach this more advanced stage at an earlier point in time? For Frankl, this would involve an effort to combine the attitudinal values with creative and experiential values; for Jung, values of introversion with those of extroversion; for Bühler, it would involve an earlier attempt to achieve different kinds of life goals at the same time; and for Kierkegaard, an earlier affirmation of one's spiritual being. In other words, should you strive towards reaching a higher level than that on which you are currently placed? Or should you live life to the full on some lower level in order to be able to put it behind you? For example, should Kierkegaard's aesthetic stage be lived to the full for as long as it lasts? And should the expansive and creative values identified by Frankl be given priority to the exclusion of other concerns, based on the expectation that the other dimensions of life will appear in their own good time?

Jung's answer would probably be that life should be lived on the level where people happen to find themselves. There is no trick by which one can just jump to the next level. Each stage must be fully lived according to its intrinsic nature. This view, however, seems to imply a way of life that can be very one-sided. An opposing view might recommend a balanced way of life; one which seeks to combine work and family life, intellectual and artistic interests, extroverted and introverted activities throughout one's life. The same balanced life all the way through. It is certainly not easy to say which of these two approaches is the most commendable. They appear to be quite different in nature and so far, there seems to be no existential theory or empirical evidence to support one of them in preference to the other. But at least we have raised the question.

LIFE VALUES, CROSS-CULTURAL PERSPECTIVES AND THE GLOBALISED WORLD

Life meaning and life values vary immensely according to the culture or subculture in which you live. We have previously mentioned Allport's six types of living. They are quite varied, but they all are common in twentieth century American society. If you look at other cultures around the world, the variation will be much greater.

In the world as a whole we see presently two contrasting developments each counterbalancing each other. One is the trend of globalisation. This trend makes all human beings on the Earth more similar to each other in questions of life values. Although the differences between the wealthy and the poor inhabitants of this world are becoming more and more visible for everybody through TV and other media, at the same time there is an increased sharing of life values and goals among the rich and the poor. To an ever-increasing degree, everybody wants the same material goods, the same cars, the same clothes, the same handbags, the same watches and the same mobile phones.

The other trend is that of cultural diversity and cultural clashes. Because the world is becoming a smaller place and people are migrating more or travelling around for work or pleasure, we see more meetings and also more clashes between the various cultures of the world. Especially these years, there are clashes between various religious groups and between secular values and certain religious values. Also, a number of minority groups in many societies struggle for recognition of the way of life they want to pursue.

Both these tendencies carry strong implications for the life values of our time and for the life goals that people choose and life meaning they search for.

The globalisation trend paves the way for a uniform culture and way of life with a high value placed on consuming and acquiring material goods and riches – a culture that already threatens the ecological balance of our planet.

The culture-specific trend with its weight on cultural identities and cultural consciousness paves the way for continued cultural diversity, but creates a problem for the many individuals who dream of an individually chosen lifestyle and strive towards the ideal of a reflected life, a life of wisdom. In cross-cultural counselling and therapy, these problems come to the fore (for just one example of existential cross-cultural therapy, see Eleftheriadou, 1997)

Therefore, in our time there is a real need for existential reflection on which values are really worth living for; an existential reflection taken up in groups, in families, among friends and in the discussions in our societies at large; an informed existential reflection questioning both the materialism of globalisation and the dogmatism of cultural specificity.

REDIRECTING YOUR LIFE IN ACCORDANCE WITH YOUR LIFE VALUES

Some people have well-defined goals in life. The meaning of their lives is perfectly clear to them as they go about their daily activities. They may have more or less luck, prosperity or adversity, few or many problems. But they are not overcome by doubt as to what they are doing and what their lives are about. They know what they are here for.

For others, things are far less straightforward. It is not at all clear to them what their lives are about. Its meaning is only glimpsed from time to time. And for some, it disappears altogether, so that their lives seem to them to be quite meaningless.

This feeling of meaninglessness can crop up when a first choice of a goal in life has not yet been made. Young people in their early 20s, for instance, may begin to feel that their lives are pointless if they have been dragged through an educational system without ever encountering the challenge of making up their own minds about the qualifications they want to have, and their goals in life beyond that. Some sociologists here talk about domestication. The educational institutions domesticate our young people – making them tame, docile and lacking in initiative.

A corresponding feeling of purposelessness may arise in the face of sudden loss or some other traumatic event in our lives. For some people, there may come a point in time when life seems to be utterly meaningless. Thinking about why they should live at all, their thoughts may drift towards the idea of suicide.

When faced with a person who cannot see any meaning in their life, an important question arises. Is it possible to help that person to find or reconstruct a meaning worth living for? Any one of us may encounter such situations, whether in the middle of the hustle and bustle at work, in conversations with friends or family members or just meeting someone in the street. People who work in the health sector and in most spheres of social work encounter this kind of situation with some frequency. Knowing the principles by which such feelings can be alleviated, may also be of personal benefit to professionals at a time when the meaning of their own lives has worn thin. Viktor Frankl has described the challenge of trying to help another person to find meaning. *The existential vacuum*, according to Frankl, is an outstanding psychological problem of our time (Frankl, 1959, p. 111). It is the feeling of inner emptiness, of occupying a space that has no value and no meaning, wondering what, if anything, could make life worth living.

As a tool in the clarification of this type of quandary, Frankl introduces a particular theoretical concept, that of the *life task*. Every person is seen as having such a life task at any particular point in time, whether or not they are aware of it. With this concept, Frankl helps the other person to restructure their consciousness. He turns our usual way of looking at life upside down and calls this conversational technique a Copernican revolution (Frankl, 1966, p. 62), thus underscoring the importance he attributes to it. This rotation of viewpoint consists in saying to one's conversational partner: You cannot ask what the meaning of life is. For you, that is a pointless question. Life itself asks this question of you. Your task is to answer the question, not to raise it. You answer it by taking responsibility for your own life. And you do not answer it in words, but in deeds.

The point of departure in Frankl's form of psychotherapy (which is termed logotherapy, logos signifying 'meaning') is that a person's 'main concern consists in fulfilling a meaning' (Frankl, 1982, p. 105). In a somewhat playful fashion, logotherapy is described as a form of therapy in which the person does not recline on a couch, but rather remains 'sitting erect but he must hear things which sometimes are very disagreeable to hear.' The client in logotherapy is 'confronted with and reoriented toward the meaning of his life' (Frankl, 1959, p. 104). The person suffering from a neurosis, as Frankl understands it, is trying to escape from their life task.

Frankl presents a detailed examination of whether a logotherapist can avoid imposing their own view of life on clients, something he naturally considers to be inadmissible. He concludes that it is possible to avoid this. The solution lies in living up to the ideal expressed in the formula 'to be human ... is to be conscious and responsible.' The objective of existential analysis is therefore 'leading men to consciousness of their responsibility.' To lead a person beyond this point is neither possible nor necessary, according to Frankl. The objective is leading the patient to an experience in depth of his own responsibility (Frankl, 1966, p. 275). That means to discover the personal tasks and personal commitment which may provide this particular person with a unique meaning in their life. What this responsibility could imply is also discussed at the end of Chapter 6.

One of Frankl's anecdotes tells the story of an elderly, recently bereaved to general practitioner who comes to him bemoaning the fact that his wife has died. 'What would have happened,' Frankl asks, 'if you had died first, and your wife would have had to survive you?' 'Oh,' he said, 'for her this would have been terrible; how she would have suffered!' To which Frankl comments, 'You see, Doctor, such a suffering has been spared her' (Frankl, 1959, p. 117).

Frankl's anecdotal narratives show a way of helping people with their sufferings. He points to the value of supporting them in their task of finding or constructing a meaning in the situation that confronts them. Faced by a person who has been struck down by illness, accident, divorce, fired from their job or suffered some other stroke of misfortune, it can be helpful to pose this question. 'For you, what could be the meaning of being afflicted in this particular way just now?'

If the interlocutor finds their situation meaningless, this fact must be respected. It would be an infringement on that person's painful situation to make even a hint at a demand that they must be able to find some significance in a situation they experience as meaningless. But if the experience of meaninglessness is met with complete respect and understanding, some glimmer of vitality may begin to flicker. When a person has for some time experienced a state of meaninglessness, the need to find some pattern or coherence in their life frequently rises again quite spontaneously. The person may suddenly begin to view the event that has unexpectedly changed their life as something that can offer a lesson to be learned, or as an event from which some other implications have to be drawn.

TOWARDS A MEANINGFUL LIFE IN A CHAOTIC WORLD

Is our existence basically meaningful or meaningless? Is there a purpose? Or is life a haphazard and fortuitous affair, an ocean in turmoil, which we can only try to navigate as well as we can? The existential theorists differ on this question.

Sartre and some humanistic psychologists stress the element of having to choose in a primordial chaos. Existence is a vacuum in which each individual must construct a meaning for themselves. What is chosen does not matter so much, choosing with conviction is all-important. One creates one's own existence.

Frankl sees the case differently. To him, the life goal of a person is not a matter of arbitrary choice. Rather, the tasks of the future already lie out there waiting for each of us. We all have to open our eyes and discover what is there, become aware of what our lives are really about and which tasks await us. The right choice is given by the situation in which we are placed.

Ultimately, nobody knows the true nature of this world: whether it is disorderly chaos or meaningful order. From an existential point of view, however, it is indisputable that the search for meaning is a fundamental characteristic of human nature. Leading one's life is like walking a tightrope stretched out between two poles, one meaningful and the other pointless. We catch an occasional glimpse of the chasm beneath, of chaos and fortuitousness. We struggle with and against other people in the hope of maintaining a balance, getting ahead, seeing a goal, finding something important, something that really has significance.

The meaning of a life is constituted by the activities of that life. Meaning conveys form and structure on activity, lends continuity and coherence to existence.

Life meaning is related to *life feeling, life courage* and *life energy*, as discussed in Chapter 1. Where does life meaning come from? Life meaning springs from the source of life in each of us; the deep and inviolable core, which is biological in origin, but which undergoes a transformation in the human psyche on its way to shining forth in our world of co-being and connecting with others and with something bigger than ourselves.

There is also a close relation between *life meaning* and *existential happiness*. As discussed in Chapter 2 there are three dimensions of existential happiness and each of them may fill your life with meaning: Bodily happiness is an inherently meaningful way of being in the world; to enjoy moving, dancing, running, sensing and relaxing does not presuppose any questions or answers. Clarity-towards-death enables you to feel the satisfaction and meaning of your everyday activities because you know of life's limits and therefore have decided to use your lifetime for the right purposes and to share your values in being with others. Spiritual happiness bestows on you the life meaning that stems from your feeling of belonging to a greater scheme of things.

To find a rich and full meaning in one's life is thus a two-sided activity. One side is to learn to cherish what is already there for you; to learn to enjoy and be grateful for all the sensuous pleasures, emotional experiences and intellectual and social challenges that life offers. The other side is to acknowledge and appreciate that there is something out there which is more important than yourself; that you may find the greatest satisfaction by contributing to the world that gave birth to you.

This connects *life meaning* with *responsibility*. If you live responsibly as described at the end of Chapter 6, your life will tend to be full of meaning. To live responsibly means to embrace not only yourself and your closest kin but also to embrace the world as such. Existential thinking is often seriously misunderstood at this point. Many seem to believe that to carry out your reflections on your own life implies that you should mainly look inward, focus on yourself as a person and turn your back on the noisy world. Nothing could be more wrong. Existence is to stretch out your hand towards the world out there. The world is burning and in need of all the attention of good-hearted and wise people that it can get. There is poverty, war, refugees, racism, hatred, diseases, starvation and giant climatic changes out there as well as a marvellous nature and lots of human wonders. In every street where you walk you may meet a lot of misery to attend to as well as friendly, smiling people to react to. There is a whole world out there calling for you, waiting for you and giving meaning to you.

Finally, there is one aspect of the meaningful life that should never be forgotten: continuously to reflect on these questions: *What is really important for us as human beings? What does really make MY life worth living?*

EXISTENTIAL WRITERS AND THEIR MAJOR WORKS

This list comprises pioneering existential psychologists and psychiatrists as well as some of the most influential existential philosophers and other existential thinkers, primarily from this century; focusing on the existential-psychological aspects of their thinking. Please refer to the index to see where in the present volume the individual writers are mentioned.

Binswanger, Ludwig (1881–1966), Swiss psychiatrist

Born in Kreuzlingen, Binswanger studied medicine and specialised in psychiatry at the Universities of Lausanne, Heidelberg and Zurich. He completed his doctorate in 1907 and was Principal at the Bellevue Sanatorium at Kreuzlingen from 1910 to 1956.

Binswanger was originally trained as a psychoanalyst, but later developed the so-called existential analysis, or *Daseinanalysis*, which differed from Freud's teachings by using analytical methods and procedures combined with a theoretical underpinning based on Husserl's phenomenology and Heidegger's existential philosophy. As one of the few psychoanalysts that deviated from Freud's teachings, Binswanger nevertheless succeeded in maintaining a life-long cooperation with Freud. In particular, Binswanger sought to develop a phenomenological and existential understanding of psychotic states. His works include *Grundformen und Erkenntnis menschlichen Daseins* [The basic structure and understanding of human existence] (1942) and the famous case story 'The Case of Ellen May', which is included in May, Angel & Ellenberger (Eds), *Existence* (1958).

Binswanger is often considered the founder of existential therapy and an important theoretician within existential psychology. In continental Europe, his work has been continued by Medard Boss, while Rollo May has evolved his work and made his theories known in the USA and Great Britain.

Bollnow, Otto F. (1903–1991), German philosopher and educational thinker
Born in Stettin, Bollnow studied mathematics, physics and philosophy at the Universities of Göttingen and Freiburg. From 1938 to 1970, he was professor of philosophy, psychology and pedagogy at the Universities of Giessen, Kiel, Mainz and Tübingen.

Bollnow strove to develop a philosophical anthropology, that is a philosophy about what it is to be human. He was inspired by Martin Heidegger and developed descriptions of and theories about phenomena such as moods, crises, human encounters, and personal maturity. His works include *Das Wesen der Stimmungen* [The nature of moods] (1941/1995), *Existenzphilosophie & Pädagogik* [Existential philosophy and education] (1959) and *Crisis and new beginning* (1966/1987).

Bollnow seems to be unfamiliar to many existential psychologists, but his existential contributions to philosophy and education are clearly relevant to psychology and therapy.

Boss, Medard (1903–1990), Swiss psychiatrist
Medard Boss was born in St Gallen and studied medicine in Zurich, Paris, Vienna and London. In 1947, he was appointed to the Chair of Philosophy at the University of Zurich.

With a strong foothold in clinical work and under fervid influence from the German philosopher Martin Heidegger, Boss developed a theory of existential psychotherapy, including a phenomenological method for the interpretation of dreams. His works include *Meaning and content of sexual perversions* (1946/1949), *The analysis of dreams* (1953/1958), *Psychoanalysis and Daseins analysis* (1957/1963), and *Existential foundations of medicine and psychology* (1994) (his major work).

Characterised by a consistent and stringently developed position, Medard Boss is one of the main figures in existential psychology and therapy and should be considered the most prominent in his field on the European continent.

Buber, Martin (1878–1965), Austrian-Israeli philosopher
Born in Vienna, Martin Buber studied philosophy at the Universities of Vienna, Berlin, Leipzig and Zurich. He held the Chair of Philosophy and Jewish Religious Thinking in Frankfurt 1923–1933 and of Social Philosophy at the University of Jerusalem 1938–1951.

Buber was inspired by Jewish thinking and developed an ethics and a philosophy about the essence of being human; based on the view that it is the dialogical relationship between people that defines what it is to be human. His major works include *I and thou* (1923/1983) and *Between man and man* (1929/1947).

Teaching the importance of community and dialogue, Buber played an important role in the development of existential psychology and exerted a direct influence on Ronald D Laing.

Bühler, Charlotte (1893–1974), German-Austrian-American psychologist

Born in Berlin, Bühler was awarded a doctorate in Munich in 1918. In 1926, she founded the Psychological Institute of Vienna together with her husband Karl Bühler, and she became head of the department for child psychology. In 1964, Bühler took part in the foundation of the American Association of Humanistic Psychology, where she served as president from 1965 to 1966.

One of Bühler's major contributions was that she developed a more positive and dynamic view of child psychology than the one found in the prevailing psychoanalytic perception of childhood. Development and the quest for self-realisation were keywords to her understanding of the human psyche. Her works include, with Massarik, *The course of human life: Study of goals in a humanistic perspective* (1968).

A leading figure within American humanistic psychology, Charlotte Bühler indirectly paved the way for the existential orientation in psychology in the USA.

Condrau, Gion (1919–2006), Swiss psychiatrist

Born in Switzerland, Condrau studied medicine in Bern and later philosophy, psychology and sociology in Zurich. He earned doctorates in medicine in 1944 and in philosophy in 1949. He has worked as a neurologist, psychiatrist and psychotherapist, and has taught medicine in Zurich and philosophy at the University of Freiburg. For many years, he was also chairman of The International Daseinanalytic Federation.

Condrau was a student of Martin Heidegger and Medard Boss. His work concentrates on similarities and differences between psychoanalysis and Daseinanalysis. His works include *Martin Heidegger's impact on psychotherapy* (1989/1998) and *Der Mensch und sein Tod* [Man and his death] (1991).

Gion Condrau evolved Boss's work with existential analysis and, after Boss's death, he became the leading figure in this area on the European continent.

Deurzen, Emmy van (1951–), Dutch-British psychologist and psychotherapist

Born in Holland, Emmy van Deurzen studied psychology, psychotherapy and philosophy in France. Today, van Deurzen is a professor of psychotherapy at the New School of Psychotherapy and Counselling in London and at Sheffield University. She is the founder and former chair of the Society for Existential Analysis.

Emmy van Deurzen's work is based on an understanding of human problems as caused by life's basic existential paradoxes rather than seeking explanations to the problems in society, culture, biology or personal pathology. Her works include *Everyday mysteries: Existential dimensions of psychotherapy* (1997) and *Existential counselling and psychotherapy in practice* (2002).

Emmy van Deurzen has been a pioneer in uniting existential philosophical thinking with everyday clinical and psychotherapeutic work and expressing this integration in clear, accessible language.

Frankl, Viktor E (1905–1997), Austrian psychiatrist
Viktor E. Frankl earned his doctorate at the University of Vienna in 1949 and worked there for many years as professor of psychiatry and neurology. Furthermore, he was appointed visiting and honorary professor at several universities in the USA, among them Harvard and Stanford. He has formulated an existentially oriented psychotherapy called logotherapy.

Frankl developed his logotherapy or existential analysis on the basis of the psychoanalysis of Freud and Adler. His theories on man's search for meaning in life were inspired by phenomenology and his own experiences from the Nazi concentration camp Auschwitz. His works include *The Doctor and the Soul: From Psychotherapy to Logotherapy* (1946/1973), *The Unconscious God: Psychotherapy and Theology* (1948/1975), *Man's Search for Meaning* (1959) and *Psychotherapy and Existentialism* (1967).

Viktor E Frankl has convincingly argued that the search for meaning is fundamental to man and should be granted a central place in psychotherapy. His works have achieved great popularity. This way, he has set an existential agenda for psychotherapy.

Freire, Paulo (1921–1997), Brazilian educationalist and reformer
Born in Brazil, Freire studied philosophy and psychology at the University of Recife. He taught here and earned a doctorate in 1959. At the beginning of the 1970s, he became secretary to the organisation Education for the World Council of Churches in Switzerland and since then, he has assisted countries all over the world in the process of implementing educational reforms. In 1988 he became Mayor of Education in São Paolo.

Freire adopts a social and critical approach to education, according to which man's life situation is understood on the basis of the tension between personal and collective history and between suppression and rebellion for freedom. For Freire, freedom is possible through learning about life. His works include *Pedagogy of the Oppressed* (1968/1970) and *Education as the Practice of Freedom* (1976).

Paolo Freire's importance to existential psychology lies in conjoining existential thinking with sociology and world politics and in devising important educational projects.

Fromm, Erich (1900–1980), German-American psychoanalyst and social philosopher
Erich Fromm was born in Frankfurt and studied sociology, psychology and philosophy. He earned a doctorate in 1922 in Heidelberg and from 1928 to

1931, he was associate professor at the psychoanalytic institute in Frankfurt. In 1934, Fromm immigrated to the USA where he taught at Yale and the universities of New York and Michigan and from 1960 at the National University of Mexico.

Fromm adhered to Neo-Freudianism and was engaged in the role of the human being in culture and society. As the individual gains more freedom, they become more lonely and alienated. Fromm wants a society that can help people endure their basic conflict as human beings: on the one hand we belong to the animal kingdom dependent on having our physiological needs fulfilled; and on the other, humans have the possibility to experience, think, fantasise and choose. His works include *Escape from freedom* (1941), *The sane society* (1955) and *To have or to be?* (1976). Also worth mentioning is *Man for himself: An inquiry into the psychology of ethics* (1947), *The art of loving* (1956) and *The anatomy of human destructiveness* (1973).

Erich Fromm is not normally seen as an existential psychologist in the narrow sense, but his theories are highly relevant to the existential project.

Heidegger, Martin (1889–1976), German philosopher
Martin Heidegger was born in Baden and studied theology. He earned his doctorate of philosophy at the University of Freiburg in 1914 and served for a period as assistant to Edmund Husserl. He was awarded the chair of Philosophy at the universities of Marburg and Freiburg and served as dean at Freiburg from 1933 to 1934. Heidegger was a member of the German Nazi party from 1933 to 1945; although this choice has been severely condemned, his work stands as a unique contribution to the philosophy of the 20th century.

Heidegger's main concern was ontological questions which he approached using the existential theories of Søren Kierkegaard and Friedrich Nietzsche, combined with Edmund Husserl's phenomenology. Thus he analysed the problem of being (Sein) and human being (Dasein). Heidegger's works include *Being and time* (1926/2000) and *What is metaphysics?* (1929/1949).

Heidegger's philosophy has influenced Ludwig Binswanger and in particular Medard Boss. Boss and Heidegger collaborated for many years.

Husserl, Edmund (1859–1938), German philosopher
Husserl studied mathematics in Leipzig, Berlin and Vienna and, from 1884 to 1886, studied philosophy in Vienna. After having earned his keep as a private lecturer, Husserl was first appointed professor of philosophy at the University of Göttingen and then, from 1916 to 1928, in Freiburg.

Husserl founded phenomenology, whose project it is to approach the thing itself, without preconceived opinions. Recognition takes place in acts of consciousness or cognition in which the phenomena themselves emerge, and the description of this is precisely what phenomenology is. By investigating these acts, Husserl believes that he can locate the fundamental structure of consciousness, intentionality. The late Husserl focuses on the concept life-world as a prerequisite for other experiences. His works include *Logical investigations I-II* (1921/1970) and *Ideas pertaining to a pure phenomenology and to a phenomenological philosophy (first book)* (1982) and *The crisis of European sciences and transcendental phenomenology: An introduction to phenomenological philosophy* (1937/1984).

Husserl's importance to existential psychology lies especially in the development of phenomenology.

Jaspers, Karl (1883–1969), German psychiatrist and philosopher
Karl Japers was born in Oldenburg and studied law in Heidelberg and Munich and later medicine and psychiatry at the universities of Berlin, Göttingen and Heidelberg. In 1916, he was appointed professor of psychology and, in 1921, professor of philosophy in Heidelberg. Later, Jaspers went to Switzerland and, from 1948, he taught at the University of Basel.

Jaspers distinguished between the practical handling of daily life and the knowledge about it that is gained through objective, scientific investigation (Dasein) on the one hand, and the existential richness of authentic being (Existenz) on the other. Especially the latter was important because this is where we find man's potential for experiencing total freedom and limitless possibilities, but also the risk of feeling isolated and lonely. His works include *Philosophy I–III* (1932), *General psychopathology* (1959) and *Karl Jaspers: Basic philosophical writings* (1986).

Jaspers developed a system of existential philosophy that is comparable to Heidegger's with regard to complexity and richness. Its application in existential psychology and therapy, however, has remained relatively unexplored.

Kierkegaard, Søren (1813–1855), Danish theologian and philosopher
Søren Kierkegaard studied philosophy and theology at the University of Copenhagen. Kierkegaard completed his studies in 1840. The year after, he broke his engagement with Regine Olsen, and henceforth he lived in isolation from the rest of the world while exhibiting a unique literary productivity.

A recurrent theme in Kierkegaard's writing is the three spheres of existence – the aesthetical, the ethical and the religious remaining, according to Kierkegaard, in a state of constant tension. The highest level of human existence is our recognition of the need for religion as a subjective commitment to truth. His works include *Either-or* (1843/1987), *The concept of anxiety* (1844/1980), *Philosophical fragments* (1844/1985), *Stages on life's path* (1845/1988) and *The sickness unto death* (1849/1941).

Even though the concepts and methods of existential psychology today seem to be somewhat removed from those of Kierkegaard, his significance can hardly be overestimated. Practically all existential thinkers are influenced by and to some extent build on the foundation that he laid.

Laing, Ronald D (1927–1989), Scottish psychiatrist

Ronald D Laing was born in Glasgow and studied medicine at the University of Glasgow. He practised as a psychiatrist and was attached to the Tavistock Institute in London from 1961 to 1967. He was co-founder of the Philadelphia Association, running a number of alternative treatment institutions for people with psychotic conditions; among them the well-known Kingsley Hall.

Laing reviewed and criticised the current perception of psychopathology and treatment of the mentally ill, in particular psychotic states. Laing's position is that psychotic reactions are the outcome of existential crises that have arisen as a result of deficient patterns of interaction in the family, which are in turn determined by power structures in society. His works include *The self and others* (1961), *The divided self* (1965), *The politics of experience and the bird of paradise* (1967), *The politics of the family* (1969) and, together with A. Esterson, *Sanity, madness and the family* (1964).

Laing's contribution to existential psychology lies especially in his demonstration that it is possible through conversation to empathise with psychotic being and communicate meaningfully with people in a psychotic state.

May, Rollo (1909–1994), American psychologist

Rollo May was born in Ada, Ohio, in 1909. After having graduated from Oberlin College in Ohio, he taught English for three years at Anatolia College in Greece. On his return to the USA, he began studying at the Union Theological Seminary. Here, he became close friends with the existential theologian Paul Tillich, who exerted a great influence on May's thinking.

From 1948, May was associated with the William Alanson White Institute of Psychiatry, Psychology and Psychoanalysis, meeting colleagues like Harry Stack Sullivan and Erich Fromm. Subsequently, he went to Columbia University in New York, earning his PhD in clinical psychology in 1949. In 1955, he was employed at the New School for Social Research in New York and taught as visiting professor at the universities of Harvard, Princeton and Yale. Core concepts in his work in psychology are authenticity, responsibility, transcendence, I–thou relations, presence and other existential categories. His works include *Man's search for himself* (1953), *Existence* (1958), *Psychology and the human dilemma* (1967), *Love and will* (1972), *The meaning of anxiety* (1977), *The discovery of being* (1983) and *The cry for myth* (1991).

Rollo May was a leading exponent for existential psychology and therapy in the USA. He was the first American to appreciate the theories of Ludwig Binswanger and Medard Boss and was able to communicate this understanding in well-written, clearly presented texts.

Merleau-Ponty, Maurice (1908–1961), French philosopher

Maurice Merleau-Ponty was born in Rochefort-sur-mer and studied philosophy at École Normale Supérieure in Paris from 1926 to 1930. In 1949, Merleau-Ponty was appointed professor of psychology and pedagogy at the University of Sorbonne in Paris and of philosophy at Collège de France in Paris. He was co-founder of the magazine *Les temps modernes*.

Under the influence of such philosophers as Hegel and Husserl, Merleau-Ponty strove to combine phenomenology, existential philosophy and dialectics. His thinking was characterised by the tension between the immediate, that is sensitivity and the human bodilyness on the one hand, and the communicative context, that is the historical and linguistic context, on the other. His works include *Phenomenology of perception* (1945), *The visible and the invisible* (1964) and *Sense and non-sense* (1968).

Merleau-Ponty has played a role for existential psychologists' understanding of phenomenology and bodily phenomena.

Nietzsche, Friedrich (1844–1900), German philosopher

Friedrich Nietzsche was born in Röcken and studied theology in Bonn and classical philology at the University in Leipzig. In 1877, Nietzsche was appointed professor at the University of Basel, but the very same year he had to resign from the position due to health problems. Nietzsche suffered from health problems for the rest of his life; this did not, however, prevent him from writing several important works.

Nietzsche's project is very much a reassessment of existing Western values. Absolutes such as truth, goodness and beauty are discarded and instead, new values must be established with a basis in man's concepts of free and powerful personal activity and the will to power. His works include *Thus spake Zarathustra* (1883/1961) and *Beyond good and evil* (1966).

Nietzsche's influence on existential psychology is indirect. His concepts about the role of the subject, unfolding, responsibility and choice form the backdrop to a number of existential themes that have been taken up and developed by others.

Rank, Otto (1884–1939), Austrian philosopher and psychoanalyst

Otto Rank was born in Vienna. He earned a doctorate in philosophy at the University of Vienna in 1912, and the same year he became chairman of Vienna's Psychoanalytic Society. For a long period, Rank was Sigmund Freud's closest associate, but when their relationship cooled during the second decade of the previous century, Rank lost his status in the psychoanalytic field. He then taught and practised in Paris and New York.

Rank is known partly for his interest in individual possibilities for personal development and self-actualisation, including the development of will; partly for his interpretation of the importance of art and myth to psychoanalytic theory. His works include *Will therapy and truth and reality* (1968) and *The trauma of birth* (1973).

Otto Rank's theories on the development and unfolding of will have had an impact on the existential psychology of Rollo May and Irvin Yalom.

Sartre, Jean-Paul (1905–1980), French philosopher and writer
Jean-Paul Sartre was born in Paris and studied philosophy at École Normale Supérieure from 1924 to 1929. Sartre studied phenomenology and existential philosophy on a scholarship at Institut Francais in Berlin. Until 1944, he worked as a college teacher in France, and subsequently he supported himself entirely as a freelance writer. In 1945, Sartre was co-founder of the magazine *Les temps modernes*.

Under the influence of Hegel, Husserl and Heidegger, among others, Sartre sought to evolve phenomenological and existential themes. In his first major work, he determined man's existence as freedom, and because of his radical philosophy of freedom, he became a major figure in French existentialism. In Sartre's later works, the understanding of freedom changed towards a perception of freedom in a social and historical context. His works include *The emotions: Outline of a theory* (1948), *Critique of dialectical reason: Theory of practical ensembles* (1976), *Being and nothingness* (1977) and *Existentialism and human emotions* (1990).

Sartre's importance to existential psychology lies especially in his emphasis on freedom, choice and responsibility.

Spinelli, Ernesto (1949–), Italian-Canadian-British psychologist
Ernesto Spinelli was born in Italy and studied psychology in Canada and England. Spinelli earned a personal chair as professor of Psychotherapy and Counselling Psychology at Regent's College in London, where he is now a senior fellow. He is a past chair of the Society for Existential Analysis.

Spinelli has adopted a phenomenological approach to psychology, which makes it possible to reconsider many of psychology's established themes and problems on a new basis. In psychotherapy, he emphasises phenomenological analysis and the relatedness of human beings. His works include *The interpreted world: An introduction to phenomenological psychology* (1989), *Demystifying therapy* (1994), *Tales of un-knowing: Therapeutic encounters from an existential perspective* (1997) and *Practising Existential Psychotherapy: The Relational World* (2007).

Ernesto Spinelli has contributed to the development of existential therapy by focusing on phenomenological questioning and relational analysis. Based in London, he is engaged in psychotherapeutic training activities.

Tillich, Paul (1986–1965), German-American theologian
Paul Tillich was born in Berlin and studied theology and philosophy. Tillich later taught the same subjects at the universities in Berlin, Marburg, Dresden and Frankfurt. In 1933, he was appointed professor of systematic theology and philosophy of religion at the Union Theological Seminary in the USA. From 1956, he was a board member of Harvard University and the University of Chicago.

Tillich works from the thesis that religious questions are deduced from man's life situation and hence they are to be considered practical and not theoretical problems. The key to healing lies in a genuine meeting with other people, which is why an interpretation of life can be achieved in community. His works include *Systematic Theology* (1963/1980) and *The Courage to Be* (1952/1995).

Tillich's importance to existential psychology lies in his development of the concepts life anxiety and the courage to be. He has been a major inspiration to Rollo May.

Yalom, Irvin D. (1931–), American psychiatrist
Irvin Yalom was born in Washington DC to parents who immigrated from Russia shortly after World War I. From the very beginning of his medical studies, he knew that he would one day work with psychiatry. In 1973, he became professor of psychiatry at Stanford University School of Medicine. He is now emeritus professor and works as a psychotherapist and writer.

For many years, Yalom has been known among colleagues and to general audiences for his books on group therapy and existential psychotherapy. His works include *Existential psychotherapy* (1980), *The theory and practice of group psychotherapy* (5th edition 2005) and *The gift of therapy* (2002). Together with Rollo May, Yalom is the most prominent American exponent of existential psychotherapy, and his books have won great international acclaim. He is also widely acclaimed as a writer of novels with psychotherapeutic themes.

EXISTENTIAL THERAPY AND COUNSELLING

The major areas of application of existential psychology are therapy and counselling. In recent decades, the psychological problems of modern human beings have become increasingly existential in nature, rather than characterised by any specific illness. This development in psychological problems is connected to the transition from a traditional and stable society to late modern society, where each individual has sole responsibility for choosing the key aspects of their own life (Giddens, 2001).

Existential views now form part of several schools of therapy, and many therapists understand themselves as working from an existential perspective. In the following, however, existential therapy will be described in its purest form as it was developed by Binswanger and Boss in Switzerland; Frankl in Austria; Laing, Spinelli and van Deurzen in England; and Yalom and May in the USA (for a description of the differences between these subdivisions, see Cooper, 2003). Existential therapy is characterised by the following salient features:

1. The therapy consistently uses phenomenological methods in queries and conversations (Spinelli, 2005, pp. 19ff). Therapists are not set on determining cause and effect and will not ask: 'Why do you think you have come to feel that way?' Instead, they say: 'Try to describe to me what your life is like at the moment, as specifically and in as much detail as possible.' Through such detailed descriptions, the therapist gradually unfolds the person's life experience so that it manifests itself clearly in the space established between client and therapist.

2. The therapeutic (or counselling) dialogue is based on a direct, personal relation between client and therapist, not a transference relation (Yalom, 2002, pp. 75ff). At the same time, the emphasis is on a dialogue between equals, characterised by mutual respect. Conversational structures where the therapist merely asks questions and the client just delivers answers are discouraged. Such asymmetry is seen as detrimental to the client's autonomy. Instead, a collaborative examination of the client's situation is

encouraged. The ideal image is that of two peers, colleagues standing side by side, seized by wonder at something they see unfolding before them; that is, the client's life (Deurzen, 2002). Yalom uses the word 'fellow travellers' to designate a similar vision (Yalom, 2002, p. 8).

3. The therapeutic dialogue in existential therapy examines the connections between everyday experiences and the basic existential conditions. In some cases, these connections are self-evident, as in an acute experience of crisis after suffering an attack, a stroke or a traffic accident, where shock and the sense of crisis automatically unleash the depths of existence. In other cases, the possible connections between an everyday occurrence and a basic category are explored in a more meditative and reflexive way. An everyday experience like: 'Oh no, I never seem to have time enough, I must hurry' may in some cases be connected with a lack of acceptance of the finality of life. In such cases, the existential therapist will try to establish an ontic-ontological connection (i.e. using Heidegger's terminology, a connection between the ontic everyday level and the ontological level of being) (Holzhey-Kunz, 1996). Such a connection will facilitate the client's direct involvement with their relation to the depths of existence. And a serene relationship to the basic conditions, such as death, is seen as leading to a freer, more open and well-rooted life.

4. In existential therapy and counselling, there is little emphasis on diagnosis. If the psychiatric system, for instance, has provided such diagnoses, they may form part of a dialogue in which client and therapist together reflect on what type of meaning one should attach to them. Also, the therapist does not normally initiate the therapy by tracing the client's developmental history, since childhood and parents are not seen as causes that have to be 'put on the table' immediately. On the contrary, both diagnosis and childhood history can easily block or hinder the client's insight into their possibilities in life. Instead, client and therapist immediately address what it is in the client's current life situation that has lead up to the meeting taking place between client and therapist right now. Furthermore, the client describes their life situation in general, including positive as well as negative aspects.

This initial orientation in the client's situation is sometimes based on a horizontal exploration of the various areas of the client's life: working life and education, family, recreational activities, personal life, etc. This exploration may be structured according to the theory of the four life worlds (the natural, the social, the personal, and the ideal), developed by Emmy van Deurzen (Deurzen, 1995; Deurzen & Arnold-Baker, 2005) on the basis of a classic theory by Binswanger. According to this fourfold theory, an insufficient ability to inhabit or unfold in one of these worlds or life areas can easily lead to problems in the other areas. If you do not feel at home in your personal life, that is if you do not have a basic sense of who you are, this will often make itself felt in inadequacies in your social communication and disrupt your relationship to your body.

Thus the first step in the therapeutic process is to describe and clarify the client's life in the present. Later on, the client's views of their past and future are included as central themes, so that the person's position in space as well as time is incorporated.

5. The aim of existential therapy and counselling is often defined as a tool enabling clients to live as richly textured lives as possible and to unfold and realise their potential in the modern world, marked as it is by dilemmas. Therapy and counselling do not have as their primary goal to remove symptoms, even though these symptoms may well be alleviated. The most important thing is that the person – in the words of Medard Boss – will be increasingly able to meet the world freely and openly. Medard Boss – as opposed to some of the humanistic psychologists – constantly emphasises that the individual cannot be viewed in isolation, but should always be understood in their relatedness, their being-in-the-world. Boss calls the ideal state of this being-in-the-world 'composed, joyous serenity' (Boss, 1994, p. 112) – when the individual embraces the world with clarity and openness.

BIBLIOGRAPHY

Alberoni, F. (1996). *I love you*. Milano: Cooperativa Libraria IULM.

Allport, G.B. (1961). *Pattern and growth in personality*. New York: Holt, Rinehart & Winston.

Amundsen, R. (1987). *Livets speil. Opplevelser på dødens terskel*. [The mirror of life. Experiences on the threshold of death]. Oslo: Aventura.

Argyle, M. (2001). *The psychology of happiness*. London: Routledge.

Benson, H. (2000). *The relaxation response*. New York: Quill.

Berger, P.L. & Luckmann, T. (1991). *The social construction of reality. A treatise in the sociology of knowledge*. London: Penguin.

Binswanger, L. (1942/1993). *Grundformen und Erkenntnis menschlichen Daseins* [The basic structure and understanding of human existence]. Kröning: Roland Asanger Verlag.

Boadella, D. (1987). *Lifestreams: An introduction to biosynthesis*. London: Routledge & Kegan Paul.

Bollnow, O.F. (1941/1995). *Das Wesen der Stimmungen*. [The Nature of Moods] Frankfurt am Main: Klostermann Vittorio.

Bollnow, O.F. (1959). *Existenzphilosophie und Pädagogik*. [Existential philosophy and education] Stuttgart: Kohlhammer.

Bollnow, O.F. (1966/1987). *Crisis and new beginning: Contributions to pedagogical anthropology*. Pittsburgh: Duquesne University Press.

Boss, M. (1946/1949). *Meaning and content of sexual perversions: A Daseinsanalytic approach to the psychopathology of the phenomenon of love*. New York: Grune & Stratton.

Boss, M. (1957/1963). *Psychoanalysis and Daseins analysis*. New York: Basic Books.

Boss, M. (1953/1958). *The analysis of dreams*. New York: Philosophical Library.

Boss, M. (1990). Anxiety, guilt and psychotherapeutic liberation. In K. Hoeller (Ed.), *Readings in existential psychology and psychiatry*. Special edition of *Review of Existential Psychology and Psychiatry*.

Boss, M. (1994). *Existential foundations of medicine and psychology*. New Jersey, NJ: Aronson.

Buber, M. (1923/1983). *I and thou*. Edinburgh: T & T Clark.

Buber, M. (1929/1947). *Between man and man*. London: Kegan Paul.

Buber, M. (1965/1988). *The knowledge of man: Selected essays*. Atlantic Highlands, NJ: Humanities Press International.

Bugental, J.F.T. (1987). *The art of the psychotherapist*. New York: Norton.

Bühler, C. (1959). *Der menschliche Lebenslauf als psychologisches Problem*. [The course of human life as a psychological problem]. Göttingen: Verlag für Psychologie.

Bühler, C. (1961). Old age and fulfilment of life with considerations of use of time in old age. *Vita Humana, 4*, 129–133.

Bühler, C. (1968a). The integrating Self. In C. Bühler & F. Massarik (Eds), *The course of human life. A study of goals in the humanistic perspective*. New York: Springer.

Bühler, C. (1968b). The course of the human life as a psychological problem. *Human Development, 2,* 184–200.

Bühler, C. & Massarik, F. (1968). *The course of the human life. A study of goals in a humanistic perspective*. New York: Springer.

Cohn, H. (1993). Authenticity and the aims of psychotherapy. *Journal of the Society for Existential Analysis, 4,* 48–56.

Condrau, G. (1989). *Daseinsanalys: philosophisch-anthropologische Grundlagen: die Bedeutung der Sprache*. [Daseins-analysis: Philosophical-anthropological Foundation: The Meaning of Language]. Freiburg: Universitätsverlag.

Condrau, G. (1991). *Der Mensch und sein Tod*. [Man and his death]. Zürich: Kreuz Verlag.

Condrau, G. (1989/1998). *Martin Heidegger's impact on psychotherapy*. Dublin: Edition Mosaic.

Cooper, M. (2003). *Existential therapies*. London: Sage.

Csikszentmihalyi, M. (1992). *Optimal experience: Psychological studies of flow in consciousness*. Cambridge: Cambridge University Press.

Dalai Lama & Cutler, H.C. (1998). *The art of happiness. A handbook for living*. New York: Riverhead Books.

Deurzen-Smith, E. van (1995). Heidegger and psychotherapy. *Journal of the Society for Existential Analysis, 6(2),* 13–25.

Deurzen-Smith, E. van (1997). *Everyday mysteries. Existential dimensions of psychotherapy*. London: Routledge.

Deurzen, E. van (2002). *Existential counselling and psychotherapy in practice*. London: Sage.

Deurzen, E. van & Arnold-Baker, C. (2005). *Existential perspectives on human issues. A handbook for therapeutic practice*. New York: Palgrave Macmillan.

Diener, E., Lucas, R. & Oishi, S. (2002). Subjective well-being. The science of happiness and life satisfaction. In C.R. Snyder & S.J. Lopez (Eds), *Handbook of positive psychology*. Oxford: Oxford University Press.

Eleftheriadou, Z. (1997). The cross-cultural experience – integration or isolation. In S. du Plock (Ed.), *Case studies in existential psychology*. London: Wiley.

Elklit, A., Andersen, L.B. & Arctander, T. (1995). Scandinavian Star. Part II. *Psykologisk skriftserie Århus, 20(2)*.

Erikson, E. (1959). Growth and crisis of the healthy personality. *Psychological Issues, 1,* 50–100.

Fennell, M. (1989). Depression. In K. Hawton, P.M. Salskovskis, J. Kirk & D.M. Clark (Eds), *Cognitive behaviour for psychiatric problems*. Oxford: Oxford University Press.

Flynn, C.P. (1984). Meanings and implications of near-death experience transformations. In B. Greysen & C.P. Flynne (Eds), *The near-death experience. Problems. Prospects. Perspectives*. Springfield, IL: C.C. Thomas.

Frankl, V.E. (1948/1975). *The unconscious god: Psychotherapy and theology*. New York: Simon & Schuster.

Frankl, V.E. (1959). *Man's search for meaning: An introduction to logotherapy*. Boston: Beacon Press.

Frankl, V.E. (1966). *The doctor and the soul: From psychotherapy to logotherapy*. New York: Alfred A. knopf.

Frankl, V.E. (1967). *Psychotherapy and existentialism: Selected papers on logotherapy*. New York: Simon & Schuster.

Freire, P. (1968/1970). *Pedagogy of the oppressed*. New York: Continuum.

Freire, P. (1976). *Education as the practice of freedom*. London: Writers' and Readers' Publishing Cooperative.

Freud, S. (1895/1955). *Studies on hysteria*, Standard Edition, vol. II. London: Hogarth Press.

Fromm, E. (1947). *Man for himself. An inquiry into the psychology of ethics*. New York: Rinehart & Co.

Fromm, E. (1956a). *The sane society*. London: Routledge.

Fromm, E. (1956b). *The art of loving*. New York: Harper & Bros.

Fromm, E. (1960). *The fear of freedom*. London: Routledge.

Fromm, E. (1973). *The anatomy of human destructiveness*. New York: Holt, Rinehart and Winston.

Fromm, E. (1976). *To have or to be?* New York: Harper and Row.

Giddens, A. (2001). *Modernity and self-identity. Self and Society in the late modern age*. Cambridge: Polity.

Giorgi, A. (1970). *Psychology as a human science. A phenomenologically based approach*. New York: Harper & Row.

Giorgi, A. (2001). The search for the psyche. In K.J. Schneider, J.F.T. Bugental & J.F. Pierson (Eds), *The handbook on humanistic psychology*. London: Sage.

Harding, S. (1986). *Contrasting values in Western Europe: Unity, diversity and change*. Bastingstoke: Macmillian in association with the European Value Systems Study Group.

Hayes, S.C., Strosahl, K.D. & Wilson, K.G. (1999). *Acceptance and commitment therapy. An experimental approach to behavior change*. New York: Guilford Press.

Heidegger, M. (1926/2000). *Being and time*. Oxford: Blackwell.

Heidegger, M. (1929/1949) *What is metaphysics*. Chicago, IL: Henry Regnery.

Hesse, H. (1974). *Demian. The story of Emil Sinclair's youth*. New York: Harper & Row.

Hesse, H. (1998). *Siddhartha*. London: Picador.

Holzhey-Kunz, A. (1994). *Leiden am Dasein. Die Daseinsanalyse und die Aufgabe einer Hermeneutik psychopathologischer Phänomene*. Wien: Passagen Verlag.

Holzhey-Kunz, A. (1996). What defines the Daseinsanalytic process? *Journal of the Society for Existential Analysis*, 8, 93–104.

Husserl, E. (1937/1984). *The crisis of European sciences and transcendental phenomenology: An introduction to phenomenological philosophy*. Evanston, IL: Northwestern University Press.

Husserl, E. (1921/1970). *Logical investigations I–II*. New York: Humanities Press.

Husserl, E. (1982). *Ideas pertaining to a pure phenomenology and to a phenomenological philosophy (first book)*. Dordrecht: Kluwer.

Jacobi, J. (1983). *The way of individuation*. New York: New American Library.

Jacobsen, B. (1984). The negation of apathy: On educating the public in nuclear matters. In Bishop of Salisbury et al: *Lessons before midnight: Educating for reason in nuclear matters. Bedford Way Papers 19*. London: University of London Institute of Education & Heinemann Books.

Jacobsen, B. (1985). Does educational psychology contribute to the solution of educational problems? In J. White (Ed.), *Psychology and schooling: What is the matter? Bedford Way Papers 25*. London: University of London Institute of Education & Heinemann Books.

Jacobsen, B. (1989). The concept and problem of public enlightenment. *International Journal of Lifelong Education, 8*, 127–137.

Jacobsen, B. (1994a) The role of participants' life experiences in adult education. In P. Jarvis & F. Pöggeler (Eds), *Developments in the education of adults in Europe*. Frankfurt: Peter Lang.

Jacobsen, B. (1994b). Trends, problems and potentials in the Danish system of adult education: A theoretical view. *International Journal of Lifelong Education, 13*(3), 217–225.

Jacobsen, B. (1997). Working with existential groups. In S. du Plock (Ed.), *Case studies in existential psychotherapy*. London: Wiley.

Jacobsen, B. (2003). Is gift-giving the core of existential therapy? A discussion with Irvin D. Yalom. *Existential Analysis, 14(2)*, 345–353.

Jacobsen, B. (2004). The life crisis in a dasein-analytic perspective: Can trauma and crisis be seen as an aid in personal development? *Daseinanalyse. Jahrbuch für phänomenologische Anthropologie und Psychotherapie. Daseinsanalyse*. Wien no. 20, 302–315.

Jacobsen, B. (2005). Values and beliefs. In E. van Deurzen and C. Arnold-Baker (Eds), *Existential perspectives on human issues: A handbook for therapeutic practice*. Basingstoke: Palgrave Macmillan, 236–244.

Jacobsen, B. (2006). The life crisis in a existential perspective: Can trauma and crisis be seen as an aid personal development? *Existential Analysis, 17*(1), 39–54.

Jacobsen, B. (2007). What is happiness? The concept of happiness in existential psychology and therapy. *Existential Analysis, 18*(1), 39–50.

Jacobsen, B., Jørgensen, S.D. & Jørgensen, S.E. (2000). The world of the cancer patient from an existential perspective. *Journal of the Society for Existential Analysis, 11*(1), 122–135.

Janoff-Bullman, R. (1992). *Shattered assumptions. Towards a new psychology of trauma*. New York: The Free Press.

Jaspers, K. (1932). *Philosophy*. Vol.2. Chicago, IL: University of Chicago Press.

Jaspers, K. (1959/1997). *General psychopathology*. Baltimore, MD: Johns Hopkin University Press.

Jaspers, K. (1986). *Karl Jaspers: Basic philosophical writings*. New Jersey: Humanities Press.

Jaspers, K. (1994). *Philosophie II. Existenzerhellung*. [Philosophy II. Illumination of existence] München: Piper.

John, O.P. & Srivastava, S. (1999). The big five trait taxonomy. In Pervin, L.A. & John, O.P. (Eds), *Handbook of personality. Theory and research*. New York: The Guilford Press.

Kabat-Zinn, J. (1990). *Full catastrophe living. How to cope with stress, pain and illness using mindfulness meditation*. London: Judy Piatkus.

Kagan, R. (2004). *Of paradise and power: America and Europe in the new world order*. New York: Vintage.

Kaplan, R.M. & T.L. Patterson (1993). *Health and human behaviour*. Singapore: McGraw Hill.

Kierkegaard, S. (1843/1987). *Either/or*. Princeton, NJ: Princeton University Press.

Kierkegaard, S. (1844a/1980). *The concept of anxiety*. Princeton, NJ: Princeton University Press.

Kierkegaard, S. (1844b/1985). *Philosophical fragments. Johannes Climacus*. Princeton, NJ: Princeton University Press.

Kierkegaard, S. (1845/1988). *Stages on life's way*. Princeton, NJ: Princeton University Press.

Kierkegaard, S. (1846/1941). *Concluding unscientific postscript.* Princeton, NJ: Princeton University Press.

Kierkegaard, S. (1849/1941). *The sickness unto death.* Princeton, NJ: Princeton University Press.

Kierkegaard, S. (1850/1967). *Training in Christianity and the edifying discourse which 'accompanied' it.* Princeton, NJ: Princeton University Press.

Kohut, H. (1971). *The analysis of the self.* New York: International Universities Press.

Kohut, H. (1977). *The restoration of the self.* New York: International Universities Press.

Kübler-Ross, E. (1970). *On death and dying.* London: Tavistock.

Laing, R.D. (1961). *Self and others.* London: Tavistock.

Laing, R.D. (1965). *The divided self. An existential study in sanity and madness.* London: Penguin.

Laing, R.D. (1969). *The politics of the family.* Toronto: Canadian Broadcasting Corporation.

Laing, R.D. (1967). *The politics of experience and the bird of paradise.* Harmondsworth: Penguin.

Laing, R.D. & Esterson, A. (1964). *Sanity, madness and the family: Vol. 1. Families of schizophrenics.* London: Tavistock.

Lasch, C. (1980). *The culture of narcissism: American life in an age of diminishing expectations.* London: Sphere Books.

Lewin, K. (1938). *Contributions to psychological theory. The conceptual representation and the measurement of psychological forces.* Durham, NC: Duke University Press.

Lewinsohn, P.M. & M. Graf (1973). Pleasant activities and depression. *Journal of Consulting and Clinical Psychology, 41,* 261–268.

Løgstrup, K.E. (1956/1971). *The ethical demand.* Philadelphia, PA: Fortress Press.

Macquarrie, J. (1972). *Existentialism.* Hammondsworth: Penguin.

Mann, T. (1994). *Buddenbrooks. The decline of a family.* London: Everyman's Library.

Marcel, G. (1947). *Homo Viator.* Paris: Aubier.

Marcel, G. (1956). *The philosophy of existentialism.* New York: The Citadel Press.

Maslow, A. (1968). *Toward a psychology of being.* Princeton, NJ: Van Nostrand.

Maslow, A. (1970). *Motivation and personality.* New York: Harper & Row.

May, R. (1953). *Man's search for himself.* New York: Del Rey Books.

May, R. (1967). *Psychology and the human dilemma.* New York: Van Nostrand Reinhold.

May, R. (1972). *Love and will.* London: Collins.

May, R. (1977). *The meaning of anxiety.* New York: W.W. Norton.

May, R. (1983). *The discovery of being. Writings in existential psychology.* New York: W.W. Norton & Co.

May, R., Angel, E. & Ellenberger, H.F. (Eds) (1958). *Existence: A new dimension in psychiatry and psychology.* New York: W.W. Norton & Co.

May, R. (1991). *The cry for myth.* New York: W.W. Norton.

Merleau-Ponty, M. (1945/2002). *The phenomenology of perception.* London: Routledge Classics.

Merleau-Ponty, M. (1964/1969). *The visible and the invisible.* Evanston, IL: Northwestern University Press.

Merleau-Ponty, M. (1968). *Sense and non-sense.* Evanston, IL: Northwestern University Press.

Miller, A. (1964). *After the fall; a play.* New York: Viking Press.

Montagu, A. (Ed.) (1953). *The meaning of love.* New York: Julian Press.

Moody, R.A. (1975). *Life after life. The investigation of a phenomenon – survival of bodily death*. Atlanta, GA: Mockingbird Books.

Moody, R.A. (1977). *Reflections on life after life*. Harrisburg, PA: Trinity Press.

Moody, R.A. (1989). *The light beyond*. New York: Bantam Books.

Morin, E. (1973). *Le paradigme perdu. La nature humaine*. [The Lost Paradigm: Human Nature] Paris: Éditions du Seuil.

Morin, E. & Kern, A.B. (1993). *Terre-Patrie*. [Homeland earth]. Paris: Éditions du Seuil.

Moustakas, C.E. (1972). *Loneliness and love*. Englewood Cliffs, NJ: Prentice-Hall.

Moustakas, C. (1994). *Phenomenological research methods*. Thousand Oaks, CA: Sage.

Nietzsche, F. (1883/1961). *Thus spake Zarathustra: A book for everyone and no one*. Baltimore, MD: Penguin.

Nietzsche, F. (1966). *Beyond good and evil: Prelude to a philosophy of the future*. New York: Vintage Books.

Noyes, R., Jr. (1980). Attitude change following near-death experiences. *Psychiatry, 43*, 1980, 234–241.

Paxton, W. & Dixon, M. (2004). *The state of the nation*. London: Institute for Public Policy Research.

Post, S.G. (2002). The tradition of agape. In S.G. Post *et al.* (Eds), *Altruism and altruistic love*. Oxford: Oxford University Press.

Post, S.G. et al (eds) (2002). *Altruism and altruistic love. Science, philosophy & religion in dialogue*. Oxford: Oxford University Press.

Prasinos, S. & Tittler, B.I. (1984). The existential context of love styles: An empirical study. *Journal of Humanistic Psychology, 24*, 95–112.

Rank, O. (1968). *Will therapy and truth and reality*. New York: Alfred A. Knopf.

Rank, O. (1973). *The trauma of birth*. New York: Harper and Row.

Riesman, D. (1974). *The lonely crowd*. Yale: Yale University Press.

Ring, K. (1980). *Life at death. A scientific investigation of the near-death experience*. New York: Coward, McCann & Geoghegan.

Rogers, C. (1959). A theory of therapy, personality and interpersonal relationships, as developed in the client-centered framework. In S. Koch (Ed.) *Psychology. A study of a science*. New York: McGraw-Hill.

Rogers, C. (1961). *On becoming a person*. Boston: Houghton Mifflin.

Sabom, M.B. (1982). *Recollections of death. A medical investigation*. London: Corgi.

Sadler, W.A. (1969). *Existence and love: A new approach to existential phenomenology*. New York: Schribners.

Samuels, A. (1985). *Jung and the post-Jungians*. London: Routledge.

Sartre, J.-P. (1948). *The emotions: Outline of a theory*. New York: Philosophical Library.

Sartre, J.-P. (1969/1977). *Being and nothingness: an essay on phenomenological ontology*. London: Methuen.

Sartre, J.-P. (1976). *Critique of dialectical reason: Theory of practical ensembles*. London: NLB.

Sartre, J.-P. (1990). *Existentialism and human emotions*. New York: Carol Publishing Group.

Schneider, J. (1984). *Stress, loss and grief. Understanding their origins and growth potential*. Baltimore: University Park Press.

Schneider, K.J. (1998). Toward a science of the heart: Romanticism and the revival of psychology. *American Psychologist, 53*, 277–289.

Seligman, M.E.P. (2002). *Authentic happiness*. New York: Free Press.

Shafer, R. (1992). *Retelling a life: Narration and dialogue in psychoanalysis.* New York: Basic Books.

Sheridan, C.L. & Radmachter, S.A. (1992). *Health psychology.* Singapore: Wiley.

Sober, E. & Wilson, D.S. (1998). *Unto others. The evolution and psychology of unselfish behavior.* Cambridge, MA: Harvard University Press.

Sorokin, P.A. (1954). *The ways and power of love. Types, factors and techniques of moral transformation.* Boston, IL: Beacon Press.

Spinelli, E. (1989/2005). *The interpreted world. An introduction to phenomenological psychology.* London: Sage.

Spinelli, E. (1994). *Demystifying therapy.* London: Constable.

Spinelli, E. (1996). The vagaries of the self. *Journal of the Society for Existential Analysis,* 7(2), 56–68.

Spinelli, E. (1997). *Tales of un-knowing. Therapeutic encounters from an existential perspective.* London: Duckworth.

Spinelli, E. (2007). *Practising existential psychotherapy: The relational world.* London: Sage.

Stern, D.N. (2000). *The interpersonal world of the infant: A view from psychoanalysis and developmental psychology.* New York: Basic Books.

Tillich, P. (1963/1980). *Systematic theology.* Chicago, IL: University of Chicago Press.

Tillich, P. (1980). *The courage to be.* New York: Yale University Press.

Tolstoy, L. (1976). *Death of Ivan Illich and other stories.* New York: New American Library.

Tornstam, L. (1996). Gerotranscendence – a theory about maturing into old age. *Journal of Aging and Identity, 1,* 37–50.

Veenhoven, R. (1993). *Happiness in nations: Subjective appreciation of life in 56 nations 1942–1992.* Rotterdam: Erasmus University.

Warnock, M. (1970). *Existentialism.* London: Oxford University Press.

Willi, J. (1997). *Was hält Paar zusammen?* [What holds couples together?] Tübingen: Rowohlt.

Wulff, D.M. (1997). *Psychology of religion – classic and contemporary.* New York: Wiley & Sons.

Yalom, I.D. (1980). *Existential psychotherapy.* New York: Basic Books.

Yalom, I.D. (2002). *The gift of therapy: Reflections on being a therapist.* London: Piatkus.

Yalom, I.D. and Leszcz, M. (1985). *The theory and practice of group therapy.* 5th edn New York: Basic Books.

INDEX

Made in the USA
Lexington, KY
31 August 2014